C|
MELODIES

by Lorna French

||SAMUEL FRENCH||

Copyright © 2022 by Lorna French
Cover image: I Wei Huang/Shutterstock.com
All Rights Reserved

CITY MELODIES is fully protected under the copyright laws of the British Commonwealth, including Canada, the United States of America, and all other countries of the Copyright Union. All rights, including professional and amateur stage productions, recitation, lecturing, public reading, motion picture, radio broadcasting, television, online/digital production, and the rights of translation into foreign languages are strictly reserved.

ISBN 978-0-573-13355-8

concordtheatricals.co.uk
concordtheatricals.com

FOR AMATEUR PRODUCTION ENQUIRIES

UNITED KINGDOM AND WORLD
EXCLUDING NORTH AMERICA
licensing@concordtheatricals.co.uk
020-7054-7298

Each title is subject to availability from Concord Theatricals, depending upon country of performance.

CAUTION: Professional and amateur producers are hereby warned that *CITY MELODIES* is subject to a licensing fee. The purchase, renting, lending or use of this book does not constitute a licence to perform this title(s), which licence must be obtained from the appropriate agent prior to any performance. Performance of this title(s) without a licence is a violation of copyright law and may subject the producer and/or presenter of such performances to penalties. Both amateurs and professionals considering a production are strongly advised to apply to the appropriate agent before starting rehearsals, advertising, or booking a theatre. A licensing fee must be paid whether the title is presented for charity or gain and whether or not admission is charged.

This work is published by Samuel French, an imprint of Concord Theatricals Ltd.

Professional Performing Rights: applications for performance by professionals in any medium and in any language throughout the world should be addressed to Berlin Associates, www.berlinassociates.com email: agents@berlinassociates.com

No one shall make any changes in this title for the purpose of production. No part of this book may be reproduced, stored in a retrieval system, scanned, uploaded, or transmitted in any form, by any means, now known or yet to be invented, including mechanical, electronic, digital, photocopying, recording, videotaping, or otherwise, without the prior written permission of the publisher. No one shall share this title, or part of this title, to any social media or file hosting websites.

The moral right of Lorna French to be identified as author of this work has been asserted in accordance with Section 77 of the Copyright, Designs and Patents Act 1988.

USE OF COPYRIGHTED MUSIC

A licence issued by Concord Theatricals to perform this play does not include permission to use the incidental music specified in this publication. In the United Kingdom: Where the place of performance is already licensed by the PERFORMING RIGHT SOCIETY (PRS) a return of the music used must be made to them. If the place of performance is not so licensed then application should be made to PRS for Music (www.prsformusic.com). A separate and additional licence from PHONOGRAPHIC PERFORMANCE LTD (www.ppluk.com) may be needed whenever commercial recordings are used. Outside the United Kingdom: Please contact the appropriate music licensing authority in your territory for the rights to any incidental music.

USE OF COPYRIGHTED THIRD-PARTY MATERIALS

Licensees are solely responsible for obtaining formal written permission from copyright owners to use copyrighted third-party materials (e.g., artworks, logos) in the performance of this play and are strongly cautioned to do so. If no such permission is obtained by the licensee, then the licensee must use only original materials that the licensee owns and controls. Licensees are solely responsible and liable for clearances of all third-party copyrighted materials, and shall indemnify the copyright owners of the play(s) and their licensing agent, Concord Theatricals Ltd., against any costs, expenses, losses and liabilities arising from the use of such copyrighted third-party materials by licensees.

IMPORTANT BILLING AND CREDIT REQUIREMENTS

If you have obtained performance rights to this title, please refer to your licensing agreement for important billing and credit requirements.

CITY MELODIES received a staged reading at the Dorfman Theatre, National Theatre, as part of the Alfred Fagon Award ceremony in 2016. Daniel Bailey was the director.

The play also received a staged reading in 2014, as part of Capital Plays Festival at the MAC in Birmingham, in association with StoneCrabs Theatre. Tanja Pagnuco was the dramaturg and director.

CHARACTERS

ANYA – 26-year-old white Romanian woman, girlfriend of Wes.

WES – 28-year-old Black British African-Caribbean man, boyfriend of Anya.

MISS BEE – 64-year-old Black Jamaican woman.

DAWN – 35-year-old Black British African-Caribbean woman.

JT – 17-year-old Black British African-Caribbean boy, friend of Cherise.

CHERISE – 16-year-old Black British African-Caribbean girl, friend of JT.

COACH DRIVER – (voice only) – white British man, 40s

SETTING

Waterloo, London

TIME

2013

Dedicated to my darlings:
Oli and Raine

Scene One

(Jazz music plays as the audience enters. A song in the style of Miles Davis' ["SANCTUARY"][*]*.)*

(All four actors stand on stage wearing exactly the same colour hooded sweatshirts (black or navy). These are baggy and not gender specific. All actors stand with their faces covered with their hoods and their hands in their pockets, so that no identifying markers of race, gender or age are discernible.)

ANYA. If I stand here, hood up, face hidden –

WES. Do I scare you?

ANYA. If I stand here, hood up, face hidden –

WES. Do I make you edgy? Make you keep your eyes on the ground?

MISS B. No eye contact –

CHERISE. No, not with me.

---

* A licence to produce CITY MELODIES does not include a performance licence for "SANCTUARY". The publisher and author suggest that the licensee contact PRS to ascertain the music publisher and contact such music publisher to license or acquire permission for performance of the song. If a licence or permission is unattainable for "SANCTUARY", the licensee may not use the song in CITY MELODIES but should create an original composition in a similar style or use a similar song in the public domain. For further information, please see Music Use Note on page iii.

ALL CHARACTERS IN UNISON. If I stand here, hood up, face hidden

> (**ALL CHARACTERS** *throw off their hoods in one motion and lookout at the audience.*)
>
> (*A strong light illuminates all on the stage.*)

Why do you think I mean you harm?

> (*Beat.*)
>
> (*Blackout.*)

Scene Two

(Lights up. JT *is dressed in the same dark hooded sweatshirt as those in Scene One. His hood is up and he is carrying a sports bag.* JT *puts down the sports bag, takes off the hooded sweatshirt and throws it down on top of the sports bag. Through this speech* JT *is doing warm up stretches before he begins a training session.)*

*(*JT *has a South London accent. He speaks fast; like a freight train throughout this monologue.)*

Just you against the bar, no one else, just yourself to push, to better, to coax, to nudge a little bit further each time. Two metres four; that's where I'm aimin'; and I can do it, I know; just give me time and I'm up there, watch.

In that moment everythin's the sharpest it has ever been. There's a tingle in the moment, an electricity that has a before and an after and just me and the bar in between. A steady elastic run up, like dancin' on molecules of air. Then the strong left foot take off; not perfect, not yet but almost. I launch myself; soar. I feel complete, wholly myself, wholly me. As if I can soar to the stratosphere, shake hands with the man in the moon, talk in hushed reverent tones with the stars that light my way further and further to an inky place threaded with diamond trails of light that seem to hold my weight.

That blue; colour of the sky, the sea; infinite things that make you feel surrounded, weightless, safe, all at the same time. Reminds me a bit of Miles that does. Just the way time seems to have a feel, a texture to it when you hear those notes. *(He bap bap ba da dows to the notes of Miles Davis.)* Dad used to play him in the old days, the good days. Used to come in from playin' out and it'd hit you, like they was bound together, meant to be; the sound a Miles jumpin' out the speakers like a man possessed and that smell a fresh-baked cakes that lingers, you know? Brings a smile to your lips no matter what kind of day it's been. Those two things are inseparable to me now coz of that. A nice piece of cake always makes me feel twitchy, like I gotta get those tunes in my ears; remember the good times.

> *(A mememt.* JT *closes his eyes as he collects himself.)*

Steve Smith; 14th of March 1993, Toronto, Canada; outdoors, 2.37 metres. Steve Smith; 4th of February 1994, Wuppertal, Germany; indoors, 2.38 metres. A proper Lege, you arks me, did the business, no messin'. Liverpool through and through he says but if you cut him open he'd bleed red white and blue I reckon.

(Really animated.) Cherise, right, she does him perfect. Can switch it on and off; got the accent spot on. I don't mean a bit like, I mean you're watchin' her right, then next minute she's proper Scouse through and through, like she lived there all her life. From back in the day that I think; all that stuff with her parents, back when they were havin' family days, good days. 'Spose it's hard for her you know, to forget that, give that up. Drives her mom mental though, the accent, I've seen her; goes proper fuckin' mental. *(*JT *laughs.)*

We all got it in us though; wantin' the red white and blue. The old flag flyin', anthem startin' up just for you, buildin' to a roar to compete with the crowd. And you up on the podium, the highest one. Wrapped in the flag, lookin' down at the other two and feelin' it inside like it's all fused with the DNA, become part of the dividin' and multiplyin' that takes things forward, that carries it all on. The red, white and blue are in it now, part of things, inseparable. We all know we got that moment in us. Gotta know that, believe that; otherwise ain't no point.

Grabarz knew he had it, you could see it in him. Way he moved; the calm of it, the confidence of it. The Smith you better watch out coz I'm comin' for that record of it. Yeah he only did 2.29 at the Olympics but after that he's gone 2.37 at Lausanne Diamond Leauge, 23rd of August 2012 that was. Smashed the record but you can see him hungry still, eyin' the 2.4 still.

Me, I'm eyein' the 2.4 yeah but I'm also lookin' beyond it. Call me crazy but I'm lookin' to be the best, the undisputed. Call me crazy but I'm lookin' to Sotomayor it. 27th of July 1993, Salamanca, Spain; 2.45 metres. Imagine that, smashin' that. World Record, twenty years and it's never been beaten. I'm doin' 2.15 as it is but I'm gonna take my time, build it up, put the work in and then I'm tellin' you; Smith, Grabbarz, Sotomayor, you'd better watch out coz I'm comin' for ya and I ain't plannin' to just do what I need to, just scrape it; I'm headin' for the stars. Watch. Come 2016, see if I don't.

> *(As* **JT** *starts doing plyometric drills with three different shaped boxes, the sound of a trumpet nearby practising notes for a piece of jazz music that has not yet been perfected can be heard.* **JT** *does not react to the sound at all at first. However by the time the lights go down* **JT** *is having to shout to be heard over the music.)*

> *(***JT*** does two sets of plyometric drills (over three boxes that are laid out in a vertical line moving from down stage to up stage – the first box is slightly higher than the second box and the third box is the highest of the three).* **JT** *starts at the first box, which is down stage and then jumps until he reaches the third,*

and highest box. He then runs around and repeats this action again. As **JT** *lands on the top of each box he recites a specific statistic each time:)*

(Box 1:)

JT. Smith, 2.38

(Box 2:)

Grabarz, 2.37

(Box 3:)

Sotomayor, 2.45

(As **JT** *runs back around and begins his third plyometric drill, the lights go down slowly on him as he continues jumping and reciting to himself.)*

Scene Three

*(Early morning. On board a National Express Coach from Gatwick to Victoria. **ANYA** sits next to **MISS B**, a Black Afro-Caribbean lady in her sixties. **MISS B** is smartly dressed in a skirt and blouse. There is little space in the small seats and the overweight **MISS B** is squashing **ANYA** into her seat by the window. **ANYA** gazes out of the window.)*

(Spoken over a tannoy system.)

COACH DRIVER. We will be arriving at Victoria at 9:35. That's 9:35. Ladies and gentlemen it is illegal in this country to travel on a coach without your seatbelt. So in the interests of us all getting there in one piece I would ask you all to belt up.

ANYA. *(looks in the direction of the coach speakers and then turns to the passenger beside her.)* The message, I …he say what? He talk too fast.

MISS B. Him seh fi put on yuh seat belt. *(Indicating **ANYA**'s seat belt.)* Dis! … Jus wrap it roun.

ANYA. Thank you.

MISS B. What ah sinting, likkle pickney laka yuh come yah an yuh caa even speak di language.

ANYA. I'm sorry I *(She shrugs to indicate her lack of understanding.)*

MISS B. *(Laughs – a high full laugh.)* What ah sinting.

ANYA. You laughing me?

MISS B. No, hush mi dear.

ANYA. But I learn. I come London learn English very good. No, well? *(Unsure of her choice of phrasing.)* I come learn very well?

MISS B. Ah mi yuh ah ask? Mi deh yah forty year nung an still caaa ansa yuh! Yuh need smady fi show yuh... like ah teacha. My Henglish arite, suh uh wi undastan... although it nuh suh gud mi coulda show yuh.

ANYA. But you in England forty year?

MISS B. Yeah, but mi hav accent. Mi neva laas it. Yuh come fi learn di Queen's Henglish. Mi neva develop wha mi madda call mi telephone vice. Mi si plenty people soun like dem deh downtown Kingston now an as yuh squint, dem change, yuh tink ah Trevor McDonald yuh ah chat tuh. Yuh ago need dat kinda vice or else nutten nah guh gwaan fi yuh.

ANYA. *(Speaking slowly.)* Telephone voice?

MISS B. It arite, yuh young. Yuh wi ketch it inna no time.

> *(**ANYA** has followed very little of what **MISS B** has said but smiles politely at her anyway.)*

ANYA. I want to work hard, soon to learn English and soon I get good job and get nice big flat with a garden I think and big space.

MISS B. Well, yuh hav ambition! Nutten nuh wrong wid dat. Yuh kip up wid yuh big dreams yaah!

> *(A few moments. **ANYA** turns away from **MISS B** and watches the view from her window as they continue their journey.)*

*(To **ANYA**.)* But some ah dem lazy! An neva duh nutten fi try help dem self. Yuh... Yuh caaa even chat propa, but yuh seh mek yuh come try? *(**MISS B** emphasises underlined words.)* All fi mi granddaughter shi, shi tell mi di odd a day, "Nanny, this revision <u>well long</u>", and my food is "<u>bangin</u>'". Dat shi tell mi di odda day. Mi nuh know weh shi ah seh, but mi jus smile an nod... yuh kno dem way deh?

> *(**ANYA** smiles and nods at **MISS B**.)*

Shi doin har exams, but shi fail Henglish, yuh can imagine dat? ... Di only language shi talk, an shi fail it! She get suh much more opportunity... more dan mi, more dan har mada. Har mada teach har gud, shi talk nice, an hav telephone vice, if shi waaa use it. But no! Shi ah chat like dem bad bwoy, bout "bangin".

ANYA. Your child?

MISS B. *(Slowly.)* No, mi gran pickney mi seh.

ANYA. OK.

MISS B. Yeah, mi daughter pickney. Shi live wid mi tho. Tell har mada she shi ah move out. Two ere now shi live wid mi... jus appear ah mi front door one day... bout how shi caaa deal wid har mada.

ANYA. So you are mother to her?

MISS B. Mi gran daughter mi seh! *(Gives up trying to explain.)* Yuh kno what? Is arite, nuh bada. Yuh wi learn quick, yuh wi pick up Henglish inna no time.

ANYA. *(Relieved that she understands more of what MISS B has said.)* Yes, I learn soon.

MISS B. Yeah man. (MISS B *rubs* ANYA's *hand briefly.)* Yuh arite.

> (MISS B *wriggles out of her seat with difficulty in the tiny space she has and stands to locate something in her bag in the overheard rack. The coach jerks and* MISS BEE *stumbles and has to grab hold of the seat opposite hers.)*

(Apologising to the person in the seat.) Sorry, di space likkle. Nuh space at all. *(To* ANYA.*)* Ah wah duh dem? Dem tink wi waaa happy stuff inna dis likkle bax?

> (MISS B *settles down again and opening a small Tupperware box offers* ANYA *the contents.)*

Yuh waaa sweetie? Eeh tek piece.

> (**ANYA** *looks in the Tupperware box.*)

ANYA. No, thank you. I don't know what is that.

MISS B. Nuh cokenat draps... it nice man, tek piece.

> (**ANYA** *breaks a bit off and puts it in her mouth unsure.*)

ANYA. *(Pleasantly surprised)* Ah, is nice.

MISS B. *(Smiling widely.)* Mi kno! Ah long time mi ah nyam dem yah! From mi a pickney ah Jamaica 'til now. Mi kno seh tuh much sweet nuh gud fi mi, but mi caaa resist it.

> (**MISS B** *breaks off a large piece and puts it in her mouth.*)

> (*Lights down as the two women continue to share the coconut drops.*)

Scene Four

*(Lights up. **DAWN**, a slimly built, Afro-Caribbean woman of thirty five, is present. She is dressed down in pyjama bottoms, a t-shirt and slippers. Her hair looks wild.)*

DAWN. And he's turning them over in his hands, examining every piece. Mangled, strangled bits of the hurdles that have been pulled apart like a mass of tiny bone hard limbs on a battlefield of concrete and petrol station bouquets.

There's a claw hammer in his right hand; I can see it moving just slightly but rhythmically, in time to the breaths hitching in his chest.

*(There is a large intake of breath by **DAWN**.)*

Watch, that's all I can do. But I shouldn't. I should look away.

*(**DAWN** stares fixedly for a moment at a point beyond the few small bouquets of flowers that are now on stage.)*

(Unable to take her eyes off the scene she is witnessing.) His mask has slipped; the emotion is too raw, naked. No polite, civilised wipe of the eyes to spare the on-lookers. Just savage. Unbearable. Pain.

*(**DAWN** breathes out loudly. It as if she had been holding her breath.)*

(There is a distant sound of a jazz trumpet playing a piece that has not been learnt quite well enough yet.*)

I stand there and I want to tell him what I did, I do but— *(cannot continue.)* How do I admit that? Make him understand? Make her look at me like she did this morning after that? "Mom" she said, that's all, one word. My eyes stay on him, his grief.

(Beat.)

Then one step is all it takes, one step and he's looking up suddenly, looking straight at me. And for a moment, a split second I... *(cannot bring herself to.)* But then "sorry" is all I can manage before I turn and run. (**DAWN** *takes a step backwards.)* Just one word and I'm back in the flat bolting the door and down on my knees behind it to keep out the look he gave me. Grateful, that's what he was. I don't deserve it.

(The light changes; it dims. **CHERISE**, *a sixteen-year-old Afro-Caribbean girl enters. She wears* **JT***'s hooded sweatshirt from scene two. The hood is up and she is holding a small cheap bouquet of flowers cradled in her arms. She moves over to the flowers and looks at them a moment. She has a South London accent.)*

CHERISE. And there she was, this girl. Just standin'. Twelve pound. She put her hand in her pocket and that's all she had. She just thought, go on then, might as well. Now it'd be all; is it all right? Is she old enough? It might traumatize her; leavin' her family and that so young. Seventeen she was, standin' with her twelve pound and

---

* A licence to produce CITY MELODIES does not include a performance licence for any third-party or copyrighted music. Licensees should create an original composition or use music in the public domain. For further information, please see Music Use Note on page iii.

her yellow sun dress on. It was the best decision she's ever made. Doing that, for everyone, it was the best thing. For all of us who came after.

But doing that, jumpin', no fear, no thought, nothing; that's somethin' you do when you're young I think. When you're seventeen with your whole life still to come. Don't have to think, turn it over and over in your mind. You know when you gotta decide? And if you go one way you're not sure, but if you go the other it's all unknown?

> (**CHERISE** *gently places her bunch of flowers next to the few bunches already on the stage. She considers them a moment. She takes out one flower whose stem has broken so the flower droops. She holds the flower as she continues speaking.*)

(She worries, that the flower she holds between her palms absentmindedly as she speaks, and without meaning to, she crushes it.) I like that about her; that she just went for it. No messin'. Never tell her that mind. Wouldn't give her the satisfaction.

> (**CHERISE** *takes down the hood on her sweatshirt. She now speaks with a strong Liverpudlian accent.*)

He was the same usually, no messin' usually. Just came out with it usually. Liked that, no, loved that. But him and me, there was mess. Lots of mess. Took his time coming to the point. Months and months and then one morning he's in the street shouting up to me, all the way up to the third floor, asking me so everyone can hear. Nan was mortified. But then she's not seventeen anymore, and that yellow sun dress; it's worn, faded and hidden at the back of her cupboard now.

When he asked, and I know it was just Nandos, and maybe I should've played hard to get, made him wait.

But I felt like jumpin', no fear, no thought, nothin'. So I did, I jumped in, both feet.

*(**CHERISE** looks down at the crushed flower in her hand and is horrified by what she has done. She places the mangled flower next to the rest of the bouquet and tries in vain to gently smooth out the few remaining petals.)*

(Grabbing up her bunch of flowers.) No, these aren't right, not for him.

*(Lights dim gradually on **CHERISE** and come up strong and clear on **DAWN**. **DAWN** is straightening up her flat as she speaks. She is obsessive about getting the coffee table in exactly the correct position. Also she sweeps her floor very carefully and eventually resorts to getting down on her hands and knees to pick up any stray bits of fluff or dirt she has missed.)*

DAWN. Yes, I heard the name, of course I heard the name; everyone did. But I... I see so many. I didn't...

It wasn't until I saw his picture. That face starring up at me from some 24-hour news channel. That angry face, that disgusted face. Looking at me, judging me.

He was right, I did put him in a box. I looked at him that first time and all I saw was the way he moved, the way he talked, that swagger. And that stupid cap. I like to think I would have been different. I like to think I wouldn't have looked away. But what you like to think and who you really are two different things.

(Beat.)

If I'm honest, really honest, he reminded me of her that first time. That's why I thought; if I can do this thing for you, help you, then maybe she... *(Can't say the words.)* It was stupid really.

I shouldn't say reminded, that seems past, over with. We're not that, her and me, at least as far as I'm concerned. Especially not after this morning. "Mom", that's all Cherise said. But that was enough. I men I rang up there straight after the ambulance had been; the police tape was just going up. But she still won't see me and that's fine, her choice, and I respect that I do. But maybe in time, you know?

(Beat.)

Would have thrown him out soon as he walked into the office; been nice of course, not obvious about it but firm. But it was that cap of his. She has one just like that. I know; I gave it to her. A load of presents last Christmas and the cap's the only thing she kept. The only thing she didn't put through my door still in the paper I'd wrapped them in; red and purple with tiny bows on each; used to be her favourite colours. The ipad, the nano, the phone, the perfume set, all in bits, deconstructed into smashed component pieces and jammed through the letter box. The crushed mess waiting on the mat when I got in from work. The place reeked of that Gucci Guilty for a month. Clearly the irony was lost on her. Even now, slightest whiff of it turns my stomach. Me and her; it's always messy. 'Spose mothers and daughters always are in their own different ways.

(Lights down.)

Scene Five

(Lights up. Night. Five days before the events of the previous scene. A tiny cramped flat in Waterloo, London. **ANYA,** *white Romanian, twenty six and* **WES,** *Black British-Afro Caribbean, twenty eight are present.* **ANYA** *still has a thick Romanian accent while* **WES** *has a South London accent.)*

ANYA. These fucking people; pushing always pushing.

WES. What?

> *(***WES** *ignores her and continues practising his fingering on the trumpet.)*

ANYA. *(Indicating.)* I have this much space, just enough that I don't suffocate. *(Indicating again.)* Only this much. Just enough so I feel always someone behind me, always in front, always beside, both sides, breathing down my fucking neck.

WES. You eaten?

> *(***ANYA** *stops and looks at* **WES.***)*

ANYA. What I said?

> *(***WES***'s attention remains on the trumpet as he speaks.)*

WES. I'm hearin' you man.

ANYA. Yeah?

WES. *(Glances up at* **ANYA** *briefly.)* Moanin' innit, like always? Been here almost a year and you ain't worked it out yet? That's just London, always will be; ain't got much space for anyone. Relax.

ANYA. Relax?

(**ANYA** *picks up* **WES**'s *clothes that he has strewn around the living room.*)

WES. One minute, listen.

ANYA. There's no space in this fucking city. Not even when you're under the ground.

(**WES** *plays a bit of the trumpet jazz solo*[*] *– he is clearly off key.*)

(*Laughing.*) Sounds like many, many, how do you say? (*Thinks a moment.*) Yes, like many elephants.

WES. (*He reaches for his dark hooded sweatshirt and throws it at her.*) Cheers.

(*The sound of drilling in the flat above theirs.*)

ANYA. (*Getting a broom from a corner of the room she uses it to pound on the ceiling.*) Every night!

(**ANYA** *swings the broom barely missing* **WES**, *who has to duck.*)

WES. Easy.

ANYA. (*Indicating the man above.*) It is fair this? Ten o'clock and still bang, bang, bang, like there is no other people.

WES. Fixing up his flat.

ANYA. Pretending, building like he's dreaming. Trying to make his tiny box a castle.

WES. Ain't nothin' wrong with that.

---

[*] A licence to produce CITY MELODIES does not include a performance licence for any third-party or copyrighted music. Licensees should create an original composition or use music in the public domain. For further information, please see Music Use Note on page iii.

ANYA. (**ANYA** *uses the broom to bang on the ceiling again. The drilling stops.*) You can't build castles in the air here. Even in the night dreaming doesn't work in this city.

> (**WES** *takes the broom from her and puts it as far out of her reach as possible.*)

WES. Don't say that.

ANYA. Why? Is true. Eleven month I been here and I am still care assistant. Every day more and more far from ever being music teacher again.

WES. You'll get there.

ANYA. You say. Sometime I think I should never have leave Constanta. I am teacher there. People respect me there.

WES. I respect you.

> (*A moment. The two watch each other.*)

ANYA. Ah, I am just tired.

WES. Yeah?

ANYA. Yes Wes.

> (**WES** *goes back to practising his fingering on his trumpet.*)

WES. Mom came round before, brought some dinner, cooked too much she said.

ANYA. Oh yes. She thinks that you starve, that I don't cook for you.

WES. It ain't even like that you know it ain't.

ANYA. Do I? Four, five night every week she cook too much and brings it here and smile. (*Takes a plastic bag out of her handbag and dumps it on the table, which is covered in* **WES**'s *sheet music.*) So you don't want this? Got it on my way home for us.

WES. Careful! *(He quickly clears the table of most of the sheet music and then removes the sarmales from the bag and looks at them and then at her.)* We could have this as well.

ANYA. Who heard of that? Having...?

WES. Curry goat.

ANYA. Curry goat with sarmale?

WES. We can start a new trend, our own thing.

ANYA. Speak for yourself. *(She breaks one of the sarmale in half and eats both halves.)*

WES. I gotta learn this, you gonna help me or what?

ANYA. *(Reaching for the trumpet.)* Let me see it.

WES. *(Won't give it up.)* I can do it.

> *(**WES** eats a sarmale.)*

ANYA. Well go on.

WES. Turn around then.

ANYA. Wes?

WES. You'll only watch, and pick, pick at everything I'm doing wrong.

ANYA. *(A little hurt.)* But only to help.

WES. Turn around.

> *(**ANYA** turns around. As **WES** plays **ANYA** listens and portions out the sarmales for them both, takes a container of curried goat from the table and places a serving on each plate. **WES** ends the solo and **ANYA** turns back to him.)*

ANYA. Still elephants I think, but not so may that time.

(**ANYA** *kisses* **WES***, puts a plate of food in the microwave and turns it on.* **WES** *watches her every move with a smile.*)

(*Lights down.*)

Scene Six

(Five months before the events of Scene Four. A single spotlight comes up on **MISS B***; she is wearing the uniform of a high school cook. The rest of the stage is in darkness. The sound of a busy high school cafeteria at lunch time can be heard.)*

MISS B. Dem ah watch mi! Mi can si dem ah watch mi. "What you say?" Dem ask mi an skin dem teet. Two ah dem ah skin dem teet like hyena. Caaa be more dan fourteen/fifteen. *(She kisses her teeth.)* Mi feel ah di Davis bwoy yuhnuh... yeah, an di Marcus wats his name one tuh. *(Thinks for a moment.)* Sanders, dat's it, Marcus Sanders. Mi kno him mada... jus fi she "hi" an "bye"; shi live near mi wid har wutliss man... thick as thieves dem two; Marcus an di Davis bwoy. Whereva yuh si one, yuh si di odda. Mi use tuh gi Marcus likkle more food every now an den, fatten him up likkle. Di mada naah feed him properly if yuh ask mi... not with him always lookin like marga dawg... yuh waaa si him eye dem open up wide ah watch di food.

But dis laas year or suh him get rude, since di two ah dem lick head, dem rude bad! Too rude. 'Bout mi talk funny. Wah dat even mean, "funny?" Dis di Queen's Henglish mi ah talk.

Inna Jamaica, pickney chat tuh yuh suh, dem get one rahtid box!! Dem not even kno weh it come fram. But yahsuh, no sah... yahsuh, deh expect mi big ooman fi mek two likkle bwoy who not even kno storm fi talk tuh mi any an any way an mi fi jus tek it!! Dem damn rude and outta orda!!

Dis yah school yah... mi deh yah now ova twenty years cooking, an serving good hot meals tuh dem. All di teachas, dem kno mi; ...gi mi ah quick smile an dem might get likkle extra peas... ah proppa "hello", an dem might get likkle extra gravy... di occasional, "how you doin' Miss B?" (ova di afters; usually mi special treacle pudding or on Friday's; ah nice piece ah apple pie wid nuff custard). Well dat wi get yuh one wid ah nice crunchy bottom, an not di soggy piece weh deh deh long time.

Ova di twenty years mi deh yah, di pickney dem really change. Yuh si nowadays, wen dem likkle wats-it-not start tuh cuss mi, an mi luk roun, thinkin seh everybody woulda business wid weh dem ah seh, but nuhbody not even business... not even di teacha dem... all dem an carry on like seh dem nuh business. Di few weh ah look, ah gwaan lik seh ah fi mi fault.

Di two pickney dem still lookin' ova yah pon mi, ten minutes now, an dem still ah stare pon mi.

Yuh kno sometimes mi suh tiad, an worn out. Today mi jus totally frustrated an it mek mi long fi home... the sunshine pon mi face ah day time... not dis, mi nuh even know wah fi call it!! ... Dem yah people nuh kno nutten bout nuh real summer sun hot!! Hot like hell!! Days like tiday mek mi think bout june plum juice an ripe East Indian mango an cokenat straight offa di tree. It mek mi long fi mango juice runnin dung mi chin wen mi bite inna it!! an june plum juice jus like weh mi mada use tuh mek. Once mi start mi caaa stop thinkin' back tuh dem times.

But all dem tings gone now; fi me anyway. Is jus days like tiday, yuh kno; it get me thinkin' an feelin' suh..., suh tired wen mi luk pon dem two marga pickney ah stare pon mi an ah chat mi an ah laff afta mi.

It mek mi think bout Cherise an how shi play di fool wen shi get ah chance fi duh something wid har life, more opportunity dan mi. Something weh mek people affi respect yuh; like dem teachas sitting dung ova deh suh eating dem lunch in peace. Dem all speak nice, an hav big job; di pickney dem neva dare pass dem place wid dem an mock dem!!. Cherise coulda did mek something of herself, if shi did work hard, mi sure of it... But shi luk pon mi like mi ah tell har foolishness, wen mi seh shi coulda be ah teacha. English maybe, or sports mi tell har, cause shi always at dat track runnin' up an down, wid har friends. Dis boy from here use to go there; duh fi him exams from laas year. But shi laugh an nuh pay mi nuh mind wen mi tell har seh him already reach weh him ah guh, suh him can afford fi play roun if him want, but shi nuh reach nuh where yet, suh shi mus concentrate on har subjects, cause shi nuh hav even one tuh har name. Shi laugh wen mi tell har bout di young girl mi meet couple months back wen mi deh pon holiday. Young, young girl yuh kno!!! ... Couldn't even talk proppa English, but wid nuff ambition; tuh work hard, an be ah teacha... music mi think shi did seh. But Cherise, shi nuh have nuh ambition, all shi waaa duh, is sidung pon har backside an laugh.

(Beat.)

But dat young girl, where ever shi is... mi hope seh shi get har telephone vice by now... cause dis city is ah hard hard place. An dark eyes like di two pair weh still ah watch mi, wid dem dutty way, fi match dem dark eyes... I don't want dat fi my Cherise. Fi dem words are things shi don't eva need tuh hear if shi woulda jus listen to mi an har mada.

> *(The spotlight on **MISS B** goes down and she exits. A single spotlight then picks out **ANYA** only. She is sitting in a chair and the rest of the stage is in darkness. The sound of a school cafeteria is replaced by the sounds of the traffic and life on a busy high street, slightly muffled as they are coming in through a window open onto the street.)*

> *(A brief moment.)*

ANYA. Wes not understand; he can't. How he understand? His English very good so he don't know this.

Some day if I not need things, no work, I stay inside. Easier I do this I think. Other day I am in the small shop across from my building; near to the lights. Just to buy food, things we eat; er, two tomato, carrots and some *(Thinks for a moment.)* some, um, you know? *(Thinks again and tries to mime the object, but just cannot get the word.)* Um, what can I say? Some *(Closes her eyes a moment to try to find the word. She speaks slowly, without confidence.)* Onion. Yes, some onion. I think this is how you call it?

Man in shop he say something, I am at the till and he smile and then say something. But I don't know what is this he say so I look at him, I ask him; "repeat please?" That is polite I think but his face it change when he hears me. He does not smile me now.

The man he talk loud to me and slow like I am child. He come in my face, close; I can smell his breath, it smell of mint and cigarettes. He speaks more and more loud when I can't understand. But I still don't know.

I get embarrass now so I leave my things, just on the counter and I walk away. Two tomato, carrots, one onion. I just leave them there. This man, the one who smiled at me, looks at me kind before, he shouts after me. The words he shouts; those I know, those I have hear many times. *(Shouting.)* "Why don't you people learn bloody English?"

'You people', I think; I am one, one person, how can I be people? I know my face is coming red and so I keep walking. When I get home I tell Wes I could not get the things but I don't tell him why; I am embarrass why. Let's order something, a pizza I say smiling big with smile I don't feel. He like pizza Wes; would eat one all the days if I let him.

*(Lights come fully up on the whole stage to reveal that **ANYA** sits waiting in the office of a high street Employment Agency. It is obvious she has been waiting a while as there are several forms that she has completed held in her hands. **DAWN** is sitting behind her desk.)*

*(Throughout **DAWN** speaks very fast. She really scrutinizes the document now and then looks around the room.)*

DAWN. An... An... what is that Anna? Yot... Ya... is there an Anna here?

*(**ANYA** does not look up at first.)*

Anna?!

ANYA. *(Getting up and crossing the room to **DAWN**.)* I am Anya? *(Smiling.)* Anya Yotova?

DAWN. *(Glancing at her paper briefly.)* That's the one. Take a seat.

*(**ANYA** sits opposite her.)*

ANYA. Please. *(Gives **DAWN** her paperwork.)* I come for job thank you, so I can –

DAWN. Before we get to that I have a few questions. *(Indicating her document.)* This says you were *(uses her finger to scan one of **ANYA**'s forms to find the relevant information.)* a teacher in, where is it? *(Reads from the same form.)* Constanta?

ANYA. Yes Constanta, Romania. My country.

DAWN. So you are –

ANYA. Constanta very pretty, by the sea with big space for beach. Many people from London come Constanta.

DAWN. *(A moment.)* You are –

ANYA. For holiday they come, you know? But only in summer. Lots of peoples for Summer. But like now this time when Christmas coming, not so many peoples. Also many Romanian peoples they come work Constanta when peoples come for holiday in Summer but then go again after Summer when there are no more peoples for holiday. I come here in London in Summer but I not go again now, even though Christmas coming I stay.

> (*Beat –* **DAWN** *waits but nothing more is forthcoming.*)

DAWN. Anna?

ANYA. Anya.

DAWN. Can I say something now?

ANYA. (*Smiling.*) Yes, thank you.

DAWN. So you would be looking for teaching jobs?

ANYA. In Constanta, I am teacher, of little ones, you know? Small children I teach to play –

DAWN. You have to write all that on these forms (*Indicating* **ANYA***'s paperwork.*)

ANYA. Yes.

DAWN. You haven't filled out most of these. Do you need a few more minutes to fill these in?

ANYA. I tell you now my job Romania?

DAWN. (*Waving the forms at* **ANYA***.*) You need to write it here.

> (**ANYA** *looks at* **DAWN***.*)

In English you need to write it Anna.

ANYA. Anya.

> (*Beat.*)

DAWN. Can you do that?

>   (**ANYA** *thinks for a moment.*)

ANYA. And you don't read Romanian?

DAWN. No.

>   (**ANYA** *thinks of the best course of action for a moment.*)

ANYA. Hmm, then no, I can't, not to write it. For me writing English not so good. Better, but five months not so long time to learn this I think.

DAWN. Five months, that's how long you've been here is it?

ANYA. In London yes, five months. I come July.

DAWN. (**DAWN** *writes this on one of* **ANYA***'s forms.*)And how good is your English?

ANYA. Speaking?

DAWN. Yes.

ANYA. Good. I learn so fast this, I take course, three night every week, see. I go here (*She hands* **DAWN** *a letter.*)

DAWN. (*Writing on her document as she speaks.*) English poor.

ANYA. No, but I learn.

>   (**DAWN** *ignores* **ANYA** *now and fills out the document in front of her.*)

Another two month, three month, my writing improve and I speak very good English.

>   (**DAWN** *continues writing.*)

Have telephone voice.

DAWN. (*Looking up*) What?

ANYA. Telephone voice, I have that one day. Very very soon.

>> (DAWN *looks at her.*)

DAWN. My Nan used to say that. Mom too. *(Imitating an old Jamaican woman.)* Dawn, when you talkin' outsida this house, you use ya telephone voice, you hearin' me?

>> (DAWN *smiles to herself for a moment and then continues filling in the document.*)

ANYA. *(Touching her arm gently and speaking low.)* But I need job, thank you. My boyfriend he doesn't work now so for all rent for all bill only me now.

DAWN. Nothing I can do. You need better English.

ANYA. I try very hard. Thank you.

DAWN. *(In her best telephone voice.)* Look, best I could offer you without good English is maybe a teaching assistant.

ANYA. A what? A, I don't understand, is teacher?

DAWN. But then again even that needs basic. Tell you what, you want to get teaching bookings you need to speak English love.

ANYA. But I speak/ some.

DAWN. /I mean properly, so the kids, the parents can understand you even with that accent. I mean I been doin' my best but even I'm struggling.

ANYA. *(On the verge of tears.)* Please for your time.

>> (ANYA *gets up to leave.*)

DAWN. You ever done any care work?

ANYA. *(Turning back to her.)* Care?

DAWN. You know old people, feedin' 'em, washin 'em, helpin' 'em get about?

ANYA. But I tell you back home, I am teacher.

DAWN. Are you interested or not? We got lots of people on the books that'd bite my hand off.

ANYA. And three nights I can go learning English.

DAWN. Can do what you like. It's minimum wage mind. Shifts are twelve hours but if they like you and you do a good job after six months you get a twenty pence rise Anna.

ANYA. No Any *(**ANYA** stops herself.)*

DAWN. Sorry what?

ANYA. *(Looking down.)* Nothing.

DAWN. Anna?

ANYA. Yes.

DAWN. It's in Holloway. Can you get to Holloway?

ANYA. Yes.

*(**ANYA** sits back down.)*

*(As the lights fade the sound of **WES**'s slightly out of tune trumpet practise can be heard.)*

Scene Seven

(A strong light illuminates all on the stage.
WES, MISS B, ANYA *and* **CHERISE** *all stand on*
stage wearing the same dark coloured hooded
sweatshirts (these are navy or black). The
hoods are down.)

WES. Speak.

ANYA. I speak.

CHERISE. I speak.

MISS B. Mi talk.

WES. I speak.

ALL IN UNISON. We all speak.

ANYA. Then that look.

MISS B. Wat luk?

ANYA. You know that look.

CHERISE. What does he mean?

MISS B. Roll yuh eye dem.

CHERISE. Knowin' look.

ANYA. Putting me in a box.

MISS B. Dat naaa fit mi... box too tight, yuh nuh si seh mi
    nuh likkle.

CHERISE. No way out now; trapped here in his eyes, in all
    their eyes. Thinkin' they know all of me.

ANYA. Because I speak this way.

CHERISE. This way.

MISS B. Because mi talk suh.

(A moment.)

WES. Speak.

> (**ANYA**, **CHERISE** *and* **MISS B**, *all look at the ground during the following.*)

ANYA. No.

CHERISE. No.

MISS B. No.

WES. Just a sentence, one sentence, a phrase, even one word is enough.

ANYA. I speak quiet.

CHERISE. I speak but not at the top of my voice anymore.

MISS B. Mi talk; jus whispa few words.

WES. *(As loud and clear as before.)* I speak.

ANYA, CHERISE & MISS B. *(They get progressively quieter with each portion of the sentence until the last part is little more than a whisper.)* We all speak, not full on, not loud, but just enough to get by.

ANYA. And every time, there it is again; that look.

MISS B. Always ah watch mi.

ANYA. Does he think I don't notice.

MISS B. Dem tink seh mi bline.

CHERISE. Does she think I can't see her doin' it when I open my mouth?

MISS B. Roll di eye dem.

CHERISE. Knowin' look.

MISS B. Dem nuh need fi seh nutten, di look is enough, sayin dem beta dan mi.

ANYA. Slight smiling mouth.

MISS B. Yuh skin-up mouth.

CHERISE. But you ain't laughin'. Ain't nothin' but hate behind your smilin' lips.

MISS B. Dat luk.

ALL IN UNISON. We all know that look.

ANYA. I hate that look.

MISS B. Ah caaa stan it!

WES. So do I.

CHERISE. So do I.

WES. *(Indicating* **ANYA.***)* Especially, when it's turned on her.

CHERISE. *(Indicating* **MISS B.***)* God, when it's turned on her. I can't help but want to hit someone.

MISS B. *(Indicating* **CHERISE.***)* Mi nuh ever waaa dem ah luk pon har suh.

    (A slightly longer moment.)

WES. Speak.

ANYA. No.

CHERISE. No.

MISS B. No sah.

WES. Speak.

    –

Just a sentence, one sentence, a phrase even, only one word is enough?

    –

Not even a word then. A noise, a single noise to let me know you're here?

(Beat – all remain silent. **ANYA**, **CHERISE** *and* **MISS B** *pull the hoods on their sweatshirts over their heads.)*

You don't speak and you're makin' yourself invisible. No one sees you; no one notices.

*(***WES*** *looks at them all and waits. A moment. All continue to remain silent.)*

(Blackout.)

Scene Eight

(Three days before the events of Scene Four.
JT, *dressed in a cap, baggy black jeans and*
a smart shirt, sits in a chair across the table
from **DAWN**. **DAWN** *is dressed in a smart but*
sexy business suit. **DAWN** *is reading from a*
document she holds while pacing the area
behind her desk.)

DAWN. *(Reading from the piece of paper.)* When I got
that job. *(To* **JT**.*)* Don't say that *(Thinks for a moment.)*
When I successfully implemented my plan and
achieved my objective of employment at the HMV
shop in Trocadero.

> *(***DAWN** *picks up a pen and strikes through*
> *much of the text on the piece of paper she*
> *holds.)*

(Still reading the piece of paper and making corrections
as she finds each error.) Bad grammar, spelling
mistakes. *(To* **JT**.*)* What are you thinking?

(Reading from the paper.) Yo, yo, yo is not any kind of
approved opening line.

JT. Who approves it?

DAWN. People.

JT. What people?

DAWN. Just people.

JT. People like you?

DAWN. If you like.

JT. Oh yeah, yeah, I get ya now.

> *(The light changes as* **JT** *begins a monologue.)*

Said he'd kick me out I didn't come here. Said I had a choice; that ain't no choice you ask me. Said no way, said he couldn't make me. Turns out he could.

(The light changes as we return to the office and **DAWN**.*)*

DAWN. Well half of this covering letter is an incoherent mess, do you see? You need to re-write it. Plain English that's what we're after. Proper English, that's the key.

JT. *(To* **DAWN**.*)* Thought I had to put myself in it, stand out. But you sayin' what I got down there ain't proper, don't make no impact?

(The light changes as **JT** *continues his monologue.)*

Said it wasn't real, wasn't proper. No future in it. Yeah okay, I'm only there weekends but that gives him somethin' don't it? Board and that, can't complain I ain't payin' my way can he? Can't complain but he does. And well loud too. A proper trade he goes, a real thing, that's what you want. That's what you want, I should've said. But he had this look. Like with mom back tomorrow and Ste out of work too, he don't want her dealin' with two waster sons doin' the hangin' around the flat, measurin' your day by *Jeremy Kyle, Cash in the Attic* and *Deal or No Deal* thing. But I ain't doin' that. I'm trainin', five days a week. Jumpin', that's somethin' to me. That's proper. I'm good and he knows it. Well he would do if he ever listened to a word I said. Got the European trials Friday. Just three more days and I'll be up there, I know it; on my way to the European Championships. If I could just... that'd be somethin', somethin' proper for him to see, proof, you know? Got the afternoon off work he said, even bringin' mom he said, if she's up to it.

Dad's the one got me hooked on Miles; got me feelin' like lookin' up at somethin' else ain't just dreamin'.

Then he does the U turn, the gotta have somethin' real, somethin' you can hold in your hands to see you through bit. Funny, when I had weekends he didn't complain as much. Now, HMV, they're goin' bust and suddenly that's my fault seems like. Listen to him you'd think I sunk the place single handed. Been a week since I lost my job and he can't see nothin' but the fault of it, the 'I must have done somethin' fault of it'. Don't watch the news my dad, says it's depressin'. And he's right. All the shop chains goin' bust and ain't no one lookin' at the people in that. The board that don't get paid in that, the TV that fills the long gaps in the job free lives in that. Lives that don't get lived no more, coz there's no livin' without cash. No one's watchin' out for it, so no one's noticed that there ain't so many heads lookin' up now. But me, I'm still holdin' on. Got addicted to lookin' up, can't stop now.

(The light changes again as we come back into the office to **DAWN**.*)*

DAWN. *(Indicates the letter.)* Look all of that, it's fine for your friends or whatever but if I am going to feel confident putting you forward for a position, and I do have to feel confident, feel sure of you. You need to present differently, understand?

(The light changes once again, as **JT** *continues his monologue.)*

JT. This mornin' I come back from trainin' and there he is at the kitchen table all "can I have a quick word?" All innocent, like it's just occurred to him. But funny thing about it is there's all this paperwork from that job agency place opposite the flats. He's tryin' to hide it but keepin' secrets don't suit him; never has. You need attention to details for that and that ain't him; I can see the agency letterhead on a bit of paper sticking out from under the magazine he's shoved them under. Soon as I sit down he's on the guilt trip, the 'what would your mother think' bit. And it's out of my mouth before I've even thought, 'reason she's in there, been in there for time, is coz of what she'd think'. Happens quick then but seems to me like it's in slow motion coz I've got time to catch the vein throbbin' on the side of the head, clock the jaw clench shut and the struggle with the right hand not to. But then he's done it and I'm starin' at him, not because of the pain so much but it's the shock; dad's never raised his hand before. Never; not to me or Ste.

> *(The light changes as we return to the office and* **DAWN***.)*

I understand.

DAWN. And re-write this. *(Indicates the covering letter.)* Something more suitable.

JT. Suitable for who?

DAWN. For you.

JT. For you and them you mean. All the people like you who approve things, say what's right.

DAWN. I'll tell you what's right. You keep this up, the back chat, the awkwardness and you won't get anything through me or anyone else here. Are we clear?

JT. We're clear.

DAWN. You got something to say to me?

JT. *(Very quietly.)* Look I'm sorry yeah?

DAWN. You can do better than that.

JT. *(A touch too loud.)* Sorry.

DAWN. Better. You be back here *(Consults her desk diary.)* Thursday, two o'clock, looking like you're serious about getting work and I might have a change of heart about you.

JT. Yeah.

DAWN. Now, as I was saying, language is the first thing, they notice how you use it or don't. And a cap? How do you think that comes across? What message is that cap sending? It's a nice cap but –

JT. I said I get you.

> (**DAWN** *screws up* **JT***'s covering letter and tosses it in a bin nearby.*)
>
> (*Beat.*)
>
> (**JT** *removes his cap.*)
>
> (*The sound of drilling and DIY as the lights go down.*)

Scene Nine

(Monday. Only a few minutes after the end of Scene Five. Night. Five days before the events of Scene Four. **ANYA** *and* **WES** *have just finished their meal and* **WES** *is back to practising his trumpet solo. It is still out of tune.)*

*(***ANYA*** *is turned away from* **WES** *and is washing the dishes.)*

ANYA. You out of tune.

*(***WES*** *continues practising.)*

When you go for audition?

WES. *(Stops playing suddenly.)* Anya come on; I'm bricking it here. Don't you have some sleep you should be catching up on or something? Give me some space?

*(***ANYA*** *swats* **WES** *with a dish cloth.)*

ANYA. Oi you.

WES. Well don't keep on at me.

ANYA. I'm not. *(Throwing herself into a chair.)* I have shit day.

WES. And I haven't?

ANYA. So you have twelve hours of 'where is that girl? Can't even speak English properly? Can't she do something about that accent? Don't understand a word she says.' On and on. And all for minimum wage? You do that today?

WES. Another month and they'll up your money you said.

ANYA. Twenty pence an hour more only? Should I get down kiss their feet for that? £6.51 to wipe her arse

all day and listen to how there's just no more space in
England for my kind. How soon foreigners will take up
all the space there is.

WES. She can't talk like that.

ANYA. Why, you going to stop her?

WES. Ain't right.

ANYA. Even Pavel, when we talk on the phone, he say like
is nothing; a boy come on his bus last week, tell him
"Can't you even speak English?" laugh his accent. Pavel
say boy standing in the road insult him, then comes on
bus and insult him more. Pavel go quiet then and say
maybe he want to shout back, maybe knock the boy
down with his bus. But he can't so he talk to me, tell
me, coz it's not a special thing; just happen every day
to him.

WES. (*WES wraps his arms around* **ANYA**.) If I get this,
that job of yours won't be for long.

ANYA. (*Pulls away from him.*) I know how Pavel feels.
Sometime I want so much to knock her down when
Mrs Murphy, she talk about my accent. About 'these
people'.

WES. Babe, this time it's regular, every weekend, proper
money too. You could stop doing the full forty eight,
just half time; go back to your English course.

ANYA. We can't afford it.

WES. If I get this. I mean it.

(*A moment.* **ANYA** *looks at* **WES** *doubtfully.*)

(*Disappointed.*) You went there again tonight didn't
you?

ANYA. It helps.

WES. You only ever bring back sarmales when you go
there. It's like you got somethin' to be guilty about.

ANYA. I don't know what you mean?

WES. I mean I keep tellin' you; that woman starts on you, you come and tell me, don't go runnin' to that place. I could help if you let me.

ANYA. How?

WES. How about this for a start?

> (**WES** *tries to give* **ANYA** *a hug but she moves away.*)

What?

ANYA. Nothing.

> *(Beat.)*

WES. So you losin' faith in me now too, that it? Think she's right; I should still be slavin' away in some bank?

ANYA. No you don't get to do that. That too easy. I listen when you tell me how much you hate working at the bank; I not your mother.

WES. Never said you were.

ANYA. Who else telephone every day and say, "maybe if you talk to him, maybe if he ring the bank they take him back, give him a proper job" –

WES. This is a proper job, I told her, keep tellin' her that but she's not hearin' –

ANYA. A job that actually pays the bills and –

WES. Okay I hear –

ANYA. Maybe you can stop him wasting his time with this silly/music thing.

WES. /Alright!

> *(Pause.)*

ANYA. No I do not say that. I the one working every day of the week so you can do what you love. Have time for practice, auditions, everything.

WES. I know.

ANYA. I working at that home twelve hour days because I losing faith? I am getting as many shifts as I can at the restaurant at weekend because I losing faith?

WES. I said I know. *(Gives* **ANYA** *a look.)* Sorry.

ANYA. How can you be jealous of a building, a church?

WES. Who's the one going for the easy answer now? And that place, that's not a church.

ANYA. On Sunday's it is.

WES. Every other day it's the Church of We Will Rock You.

ANYA. Don't mock me.

WES. Don't cut me out then.

ANYA. You're being like a child.

WES. Am I?

ANYA. Yes Wes.

(A moment. **WES** *watches* **ANYA.***)*

WES. You go there; some theatre cum church at weekends, every time that woman starts spreading her poison. Take tonight; it's Monday night; that place is nothing but a building tonight, a theatre, nothing special about it, no church vibe going on but you'd rather go and cry your heart out in that lobby full of strangers waiting to see some sad Queen tribute show than come home to me. Tell me, what does that say about us?

ANYA. *(Really angry now.)* It say I have a life before this, before you. A life in Romania with my family where we everyone go church together every Sunday for years and years. Years and years happy memories, silly memories that make me smile. But I am part of things then, understanding things then, not on the outside looking in then.

WES. Not like now?

(**ANYA** *keeps her eyes on the ground.*)

Do you want to go back home, is that it?

ANYA. No. I just miss them. Going there make me feel closer I think.

WES. Ok. Well maybe, if you miss them, your family and that, speak to them; they could come for a holiday, a week or so? Would that help?

ANYA. This is not a good idea.

WES. Why?

ANYA. They cannot afford this. We cannot afford.

WES. If I do well at this audition Friday night then maybe I could chip in too; maybe pay for your parents' flight?

ANYA. You're dreaming Wes; they won't come to here.

WES. I don't understand what you want then.

ANYA. I want you.

WES. *(Grins at her.)* Look give me your parents' number, I'll talk to them, invite them for a visit, maybe then –

ANYA. *(She kisses* **WES** *full on the lips hard.)* Leave it ok? For me? And you're right. Next time Mrs Murphy she is saying things I come home to you, I promise. No, what did you say? Church cum theatre? None of that for me. Just you, ok?

WES. Yeah?

ANYA. Yes.

WES. Even if I'm just an out of work musician with big dreams.

(**WES** *moves towards* **ANYA** *and she does not move away.*)

ANYA. Especially then.

(**ANYA** *allows* **WES** *to take her in his arms and lift her off her feet. She kisses him and the two collapse into chairs afterwards.*)

You cursed like man upstairs. Cursed with dreaming. My mind it has no space for dreams anymore. So you need to be dreaming for the both of us.

WES. Good job, nice big flat with a garden maybe and big space. Remember? Nothin' wrong with dreams. I'm gonna get this gig if it kills me. Listen.

(**WES** *goes to start playing*[*] *and* **ANYA** *turns her back on him.* **WES** *stops.*)

Turn around?

ANYA. (*Turning back to him.*) But you always say/ don't look.

WES. /Go on.

(**ANYA** *turns.* **WES** *plays for a few moments and* **ANYA** *watches him.*)

ANYA. Stop. Can I Just –

WES. (*Laughing.*) You can't help yourself.

(**ANYA** *is a little embarrassed.*)

ANYA. Okay, so like this. (**WES** *holds the trumpet and* **ANYA** *places his fingers in the right positions.*) Keep fingers close to buttons. Space between nice and tight. And

---

[*] A licence to produce CITY MELODIES does not include a performance licence for any third-party or copyrighted music. Licensees should create an original composition or use music in the public domain. For further information, please see Music Use Note on page iii.

you know with Miles you gotta really feel the music, get inside it; especially when you playing our song.

> (**WES** *plays the first phrase again; there is a definite improvement in the music.* **WES** *gives* **ANYA** *a look.*)

WES. I been trying to get it right all day. What can't you play?

ANYA. What? Trumpet almost official Romanian instrument.

WES. Yeah?

ANYA. Of course. *(She gives* **WES** *a kiss.)* And don't worry; I am good for the teaching only not so much the playing. Playing gives me nerves.

WES. *(WES entwines his fingers with* **ANYA***'s.)* Difference is it makes me stand ten feet tall when I'm doin' it with all I got; doin' it right. Want to get our song exactly right. Every note perfect; like the night we met. Band playin' *Sanctuary*, almost like Miles had come down to give them a hand. Almost as good as him. But me, I don't want to be almost, I wanna be there, on it, like I'm channellin' Miles, gone back in time and am as close to him as anyone's ever got.

> (**WES** *plays the first phrase again; this time it is perfect.*)

(Kisses her.) Believe yeah, you're gonna make a great music teacher one day soon; kids won't know what hit 'em.

ANYA. *(Kisses* **WES** *back.)* There you go dreaming again.

WES. Somethin' wrong with that? Ain't there just a little space for it? Your perfect English telephone voice calls out to the children. The whole class turns to listen to the teacher. Open faces, all of them; not screwed up because they can't understand your words. Then all playing together; playing beautiful music you taught them.

ANYA. You think?

> (ANYA *breaks the last sarmale in half; she eats one half and gives the other half to* WES, *who eats it also.*)

WES. I know.

> (WES *begins to play again.*[*] *The first phrase is perfect but as he continues he is almost there but still has a few bum notes. Almost immediately banging from the flat above is heard. As the lights go down* WES *continues playing the full piece of music over the sound of the man above them drilling and banging. The music and the DIY noises compete with each other.*)

---

[*] A licence to produce CITY MELODIES does not include a performance licence for any third-party or copyrighted music. Licensees should create an original composition or use music in the public domain. For further information, please see Music Use Note on page iii.

Scene Ten

(Early Wednesday morning. **CHERISE** *is present. She is dressed in sports gear and has a sports bag over one shoulder.)*

CHERISE. You know how you tell yourself 'it don't matter, I'm only young; I got time?' Time to do all the things I wanna do, even though really, you know you're just fuckin' dreamin'? You know how you stop yourself, say, 'that ain't me, how could I do that?' Him, he never stops ya, never says, 'who do you think you are thinkin' you can do that?' Never stops ya dreamin'.

Coz that's what it is really. He says it isn't but I know, well thought I did. All this runnin', trainin', every week day mornin', 'til I think my heart will just burst. What is that about but dreamin'?

Arms pumpin', legs flyin', tastin' blood but feelin' pure, new, you know? Like you can do anythin', go anywhere. Early mornin', cold, dark and secret. Our time. Him and me, no one else in the world. I love that he doesn't mind it's just the two of us. Six months and I haven't missed a single mornin'.

We go up there, all the way up there, coz he wants all that, know he does. Pretends he doesn't but I can see it in him. The way he stands up at the start. Dead straight, his full height; like there he can, there he doesn't have to slouch, try to blend in, pretend he doesn't care, doesn't try hard. There he can really try. No one's watchin' so he can go all out, stop bein' half-arsed and too scared to dare say it. There he dares, says, "I want. This is me and this is what I want. I'll work for it, yeah course, work hard for it, but I will get it". I love him for that.

High jump's his thing. Says he's gonna jump 2.15, maybe even 2.16 if he really pushes it. It's the trials for the European Junior Championships on Friday; he'll make the British team with a jump like that no problem.

See I thought I knew what we was doin'. We was goin' up there to that place in Hampstead, trainin' our hearts out every mornin', lookin' around up there and just dreamin', doin' the what if? You know? That was as far as it went I thought. But JT, he's really doin' it; he's actually got a trial Friday, and the guy who's been coachin' him says he could even get sponsorship if he makes the team. And I know JT; he'll make it.

Don't know why he bothers with me really. Coz I'm a dickhead see, always have been. People who know me; for them that's just my name. And don't get me wrong, I don't disagree, that's not it. Coz well if you look at the evidence they ain't wrong.

Failed most of my mocks last year, even English and I'm s'posed to be good at that. Didn't put the work in I s'pose, didn't see the point then. Gran was fuming. Has always had this crazy idea I'd be an English teacher see, Gran and Mom both. Could see Gran all but wailin' down the phone to Mom when my results came, like she thought I'd lost my hearin' or somethin'. Everyone in the flats must've heard; she was that loud. 'Dat girl, lazy, jus sit down an' laugh! Dat's all she good for.' Anyway, JT comes round coz he's heard all the shoutin' from next door, I could've died when Gran just come out with it, like she don't care who she spreadin' my business to. 'Dat girl, dumb as a piece a wood' she said and laughed. JT didn't laugh. He just said really quiet, kind of almost under his breath, "Cherise ain't dumb". Way he said it; Gran gave him this look. She didn't say anything else after that; not about how dumb I am anyway. And that was it; he started tutorin' me, didn't ask him like he just came round to my Gran's one night, all his GCSE books under his arm. Made me promise I'd stop bunkin' off to come and see him trainin' in the day too. Bit gutted about that actually. Only lets me come in the mornin' before school now, totally deafs me out for days if I bunk off and just turn up. So there's no point doin' that. I'm on for mostly As and Bs now if I keep on like this; Miss Thompson told me the other week. Haven't told Gran; want to see her face when the results come out. Then I'll 'jus sit down an' laugh' for real at the shock on her face.

Few weeks ago, we're goin' up the little shop over the road from the flats; JT and me, when someone shouts, "Oi, dickhead", and I turn round. Spin on my heel, don't even think about it, just lookin' behind at who's callin'.

"Why d'ya do that?" He says.

"What?"

"Let 'em call you that? It's not on callin' you that".

He don't get it though, no one means any harm by it; it's just kinda what people call me. What I don't get is why he gives a shit. First I thought he'd guessed I fancied him when he started lettin' me train with him and that. But he never said a word about it. Kept me up loads a nights worryin' what he was gonna come out with though. Then I hoped he might ask me out, you know when he started tutorin' me, but it's been six months and he ain't even noticed me like that.

(Quickly checks her watch.) Goin' on for quarter past, he's always here by five most days. But I 'spose maybe with his mom comin' out of that place today he's got too much on.

> *(**CHERISE** looks up the street to see if **JT** is coming. She takes out her phone and checks for a message.)*

Coulda WhatsApped me though. Let me know so I'm not standin' in the bus station like a dick head.

(**CHERISE** *checks up the street again for* **JT**.)

(*Relieved.*) Here he is.

(**CHERISE** *lifts her hand to wave to* **JT** *excitedly but after a moment she sees something that makes her drop her hand.*)

Oi, Marcus stop messin' with him! Darren that ain't your cap. I know it ain't. I know it ain't coz I gave it to him! Take it off! I swear to God you pair a idiots better loose him or I'll, I'll (*Hesitates.*)

I pick up a rock. The look on their faces. Darin' me, thinkin' I won't. Marcus nicks JT's trainers, right off his feet in the middle of the street. I throw the rock. It hits Marcus in the middle of his chest. Six pairs of eyes on me then, boring into me with the shock of it.

"Bitch!" Marcus shouts.

"Crazy bitch". Darren says. "That how you like your women JT? Crazy like your mom?"

Darren spits at me then, throws the cap into the street and the two of them leave, not running, just sniggerin' and messin' about like it's all a big joke.

CHERISE. JT, you ok?

JT. Why'd you have to do that?

CHERISE. I was tryin' to help.

JT. You think you did?

CHERISE. Sorry man OK?

(*Beat.*)

JT?

(*Beat.*)

Those idiots, what they said; your mom ain't crazy.

JT. Ain't she?

CHERISE. Nobody thinks that.

> *(Beat.)*

   I don't think that.

JT. Why not?

CHERISE. coz.

JT. You really are a dick head then ain't you?

> *(Lights down gradually.)*

Scene Eleven

(Lights up. Thursday afternoon. **JT** *and* **DAWN** *are both in* **DAWN**'s *office.* **DAWN** *is dressed in the same smart outfit, while* **JT** *has a cheap suit on instead of his jeans and smart shirt from Scene Eight.* **JT** *does not have his baseball cap on.* **JT** *sits in a chair opposite* **DAWN** *and hands her a piece of A4 paper from the sports bag he is carrying.)*

*(***DAWN*** studies the paper a moment while* **JT** *waits.)*

(Both characters face each other while speaking but they voice monologues which comment on the other.)

DAWN. It's a question of –

JT. You people, you know. Her sayin' dat to me. *(Getting up and leaning across the table into* **DAWN**'s *face.)* How you gonna say dat to me? *(***JT*** sits back down.)* You don't know me. You in your Primarni suit givin' it *(Makes a hand gesture to indicate talking a lot.)* all that.

DAWN. bucking up your ideas. What you talk on road is all well and good but is no use for any interview I send you on understand?

JT. I ain't deaf, though you'd think I am the way this one's goin' on. How many times you gonna say the same thing? *(To* **DAWN**.*)* I get ya but can I arks –

DAWN. Sorry?

JT. Can I arks –

DAWN. Sorry, what?

JT. I just want to arks you –

DAWN. Let me *(Emphasises her pronunciation of the underlined words.)* <u>ask</u> you a question. What does <u>arks</u> say to an employer do you think?

JT. My girl sitting with her nice smooth human hair weave and her natural side burns goin' on like she's some posh bird who swallowed a dictionary. But I ain't dumb, I see the act, the trying bare hard but not quite making the grade if you *(Emphasises his pronunciation of the underlined word.)* <u>arks</u> me.

DAWN. *(Glancing over* **JT***'s covering letter once more quickly.)* The letter looks good enough, it's –

JT. What you want; what they tell you is the right thing?

DAWN. You just need to tweek it –

JT. Yeah seen. Take out every trace of what I'm about then it's good to go, right?

DAWN. Take out this sport stuff, high jump all that, the detail, it's not relevant.

JT. Is to me.

DAWN. *(Stops a moment and looks at him.)* Jeremy, do you actually want a job?

JT. Course.

DAWN. Why?

JT. Money innit?

DAWN. *(Unimpressed.)* That it?

JT. No.

DAWN. So?

JT. Just.

(Beat.)

DAWN. *(Handing back* JT*'s covering letter.)* Look I don't think this is going to work. I think another agency might be –

JT. No I'm sorry I need a job, whatever you want, I'll do it. You want high jump out of my letter, I'll take it out yeah?

DAWN. I'm not sure about you but –

JT. I'm <u>askin'</u> you?

DAWN. You understand this is my reputation right? I send someone out there and they mess around one of my clients and that's me finished with that company. I send someone out there who messes up and they won't trust my judgement. Once trust is lost, there's no second chance.

JT. I get it. You can trust me.

DAWN. Yeah?

JT. Yeah.

> *(Beat.)*

Hand over my passport and she's really lookin'. Lookin' at the dumb photo dad made me get when I was still a kid. She's starin' at me hard like she don't see a connection between the me sittin' here and the me in the photo.

DAWN. Picture looks hopeful, young and keen but –

JT. Still starin'.

DAWN. That doesn't last; can't, not the way things are. I remember seeing a picture of my mom just like that once; her face staring into the camera proud and young and full of hope. My brothers and I we used to search through the drum she brought with her when she came. For us it was like a dressing up box from a time so long ago that we never knew it; couldn't know it, except through stories. But stories that seemed to us more like made up tales to pass the time during long summer holiday days when it was raining outside rather than truth. Mom's truth; her experience was so different to ours that I looked at her sometimes like a stranger come from a far off land to the place where my brothers and I began with only an interpreter that was occasionally ineffective to bridge the gap. When she told us stories we would all sit at her feet and listen eagerly to feel some connection or closeness to what she described. But I could see her face fall just a fraction when a translation went awry and words familiar to her from birth had to be defined and explained for her own children who had never heard them. Or the irritation when disbelieving laughs filled the air as we found humour in what for her was just a shared everyday normal existence but we interpreted as a level of poverty our young lives had not seen and so could not comprehend. I could see she felt the distance between us then, as a tangible thing; a bitter pill because of choices made long ago, and so did I.

But on one day, the last one of the school holidays, my brothers and I were searching through her things; we always treated her drum like a treasure hunt. That day we made the most exciting find of our young lives. A passport wrapped in a little summer dress. I am not sure now but it might have been yellow I think, or was it cream? That passport picture; our mother looking impossibly young, impossibly hopeful, impossibly free, was a revelation for us. How could this other person, this carefree looking teenager, also be our mother? Our mother who was always so stern. Our mother who was always so anxious that we children behave properly, mimic the Londonness of the city where we were born and not the otherness that she felt in the tales she told. Our mother who always placed her open free island life in opposition to our British boxed in, close city existence. The two did not mix well she said, you were one or the other. And she knew which she wanted from us: "My babies, you make sure you speak proper", she said over and over. "Don't talk like me, I only ever want to hear your telephone voices, you hearin' me?"

In my 9-year-old mind I think I wanted to try to bridge the gap that opened up between mom and us children when she spoke of life in Jamaica; not to just hear about it but to feel how she felt. So when we found the best treasure of all, every night after that I'd sneak out of bed in my little box room at the top of the house, when everyone was asleep. I'd tiptoe down both sets of stairs to the cellar and slip the dress on. It was far too big for my tiny frame but that didn't matter. I imagined myself into the tales mom had told and felt like I was right beside her as she collected wood for the stove, rode the donkey to the farm, and drank water from the river behind the house, in a little green plastic cup that her dad had given her for her own. I was with her on a day when she and her eight brothers and sisters played forts up in the country for hours and then stretched out in the sun and scared each other with stories of duppies. I sat at her side in the little church a mile from the house every Sunday and I slept next to her in the bed she shared with her four sisters, in such sweltering temperatures that they always slept with the window open, even though most of them were terrified of lizards coming in.

After a week of my secret night time travels to the place my mother was born dad caught me in the cellar and ordered me to get to bed. I dared to sneak back one day after school months later but the drum was nailed shut. I haven't seen that dress since.

JT. Wants me to erase myself, this one. Take all of me out of the covering letter; become someone else. But I ain't doin' that. There's gotta be a bit of you in there somewhere don't there? Bit a personality. Otherwise ain't no point is there? That's what depression's like I reckon, just like that. That letter she's askin' for; there's none of you left; turns you into a different person.

DAWN. A week out of university and the first interview I got was for this place. I was so excited and terrified. Thing was though, as it's coming to a close it's, "oh, where are your parents from?" She asks me that nice and conversational; smiling into my face like it's the most natural question in the world. "Why?" I ask her, irritated now. No not irritated, angry, really angry. "I thought this was about me," I say, trying to keep my voice even and calm. "Of course, of course", she tells me flashing her sweetest smile. But she's still waiting for an answer.

Wait, I think and sit looking at her.

JT. With depression you ain't gettin' out of hospital until some doctor somewhere, doesn't even know you, decides it's OK. Says you're thinkin' right now, doin' the right things now. All he really means is that you're thinkin' and doin' approved things; what the doctors have decided are the right things to be thinkin' and doin', because that's what most of the other people in the world that they know are thinkin' and doin'. But how do they know that's right? What if there are other people these doctors don't know who are doin' other things, thinkin' other things, things that make sense to them? Are they all crazy?

DAWN. "Jamaica", I say eventually, "my parents are Jamaican". "Oh I love that rice and peas", she says, like it's not the most patronising thing in the world. "Oh and that hot pepper sauce, far too hot for me", and there it is again, another one of those sickly sweet smiles. I'm in danger of getting diabetes here. But I can see she's calmer now because in her mind I've just jumped head first into the box filled with Jamaican rum, rice and peas, curry goat, dreadlocks and reggae that is specially reserved for people like me in the minds of people like her. I resist the strong urge to ask her where her parents are from.

JT. Gettin' out of hospital is all about fittin' in that narrow box the doctors have decided on. The box most people in the world have hacked off their jagged edges, redefined their world view to fit snuggly into. The terrible box makes you less and less you but if that will prove you sane that's enough for most.

DAWN. I just smiled, nodded and let her put me in her box. Cherise gets angry when I do that, calls it my 'act', but for me, if it gets me what I want in the end, I can't complain.

JT. My girl's tryin' to get me into a box too; one she can deal with; one that's approved. Same one dad's got reserved for me coz he's scared I got a little bit a mom's jagged edges in me. I keep tellin' him jumpin' is all I'm doin' but he's nervous, can see it in him. He doesn't know anyone in a box where jumpin' can be contained and made to fit so he's on the drinkin' more than usual, the watchin' me like a hawk for the mom in me he's afraid is waitin' just below the skin. He's on the threatenin' to kick me out if I don't get work soon to help with the bills now mom's back and he's had to go part time at work. Thinks gettin' a job full time might get the jumpin' out of me.

DAWN. *(To* **JT.***)* I'm giving you one chance OK? But remember, no turning up late every morning; it's seven a.m., not five past with a breeze in, head down no eye contact, like a few minutes don't matter, not ten past with an excuse that changes every day. And no bad language, no aggressive behaviour yes?

JT. *(To* **DAWN.***)* Everybody get a warning so specific?

DAWN. *(To* **JT.***)* If I think it's required.

(A moment. **JT** *gives* **DAWN** *a look as he tries to control himself.)*

JT. My girl's forgotten who she is man. Does she chat like this at home? Walk around with her nose in the air? Nah man, she might be about that but I ain't. This ain't my thing. I can't bury myself under a mask of suited and booted fakery with a posh voice that ain't mine and ain't never gonna be. Not when I got my thing, been workin' at it. 2.16 I jumped this mornin', personal best that, gonna blow away the competition this time tomorrow.

> (**JT** *starts undoing his tie with one hand as he talks.*)

After that the sponsors'll be linin' up. I'll be payin' my way and then some, watch. Might even get mom some of those fancy Wes Oliver baking trays she was on about last night. Been gone eight months, back a day and the only thing she can talk about is bloody baking trays. But still, better than the silence I 'spose. Better than the silence and the non-stop tears I 'spose. Better than the silence and the non-stop tears and the can't get out of bed I 'spose. Better than the silence and the non-stop tears and the can't get out of bed and the fistfuls of Paracetemol I 'spose.

> (**JT** *takes his cap out of his bag and puts it on. He gets up from the table and goes to walk out.*)

DAWN. *(Calling after him.)* Jeremy, I've lined up an interview for you, a care home in Holloway!

JT. *(Kisses his teeth.)* It's JT man.

DAWN. I'm not calling you that.

JT. Just coz I got a cap on my head and don't speak posh like you don't mean I ain't got sense enough to see when someone's treating me like a dick head.

DAWN. I won't be spoken to –

JT. Nah man, you gonna deny it? You had me in that yoof
box you carry around in your head from the first time
I come in here. All because I wear a cap, don't chat the
right way and don't look like you.

DAWN. I wouldn't do –

JT. You really gonna stand there and deny it?

DAWN. I –

JT. What?

> (JT *looks* DAWN *up and down with disgust.*)

That's what I thought.

> (JT *exits.*)

> (DAWN *sits down shocked and troubled by*
> JT'*s outburst.*)

> (*Lights down.*)

Scene Twelve

*(Lights up. Late Thursday evening. The stage
is in darkness except a single spotlight on
WES. **WES** has a dark hooded jacket on. The
hood is up.)*

WES. Everything's loud and hot and frantic. I close my eyes,
just for a moment and stand stock still. Right there, in
the middle of it all; like one of those wind-up toys you
get when you're a kid, the kind that stop mid gesture,
an arm or a leg stickin' up like someone somewhere's
pressed pause. Need to gather my thoughts, make
sense of another knock back, another 'it's good son,
but not good enough'. Gotta keep up the smile though;
through it all. The lying smile that says ah it's cool, I
didn't really put that much into it, didn't stay up most
nights the last two weeks, 'til the early hours, the no
one sees this time of night hours. No, not me, I'm not
that dedicated, don't want every single note to roll off
my horn like a drop of pure honey I'm pouring into
your ears; the smoothest, the truest, the rightest thing
you ever heard. Nah, me? I'm too laid back for that. All
that my smile's sayin' while I'm watchin' this guy talkin',
givin' me the brush off but inside I'm wantin' to knock
his teeth down his throat. I'm out of there now but I
can still feel my hands wanting to clench into fists. So
I'm takin' a moment.

I open my eyes and boom; there she is. Right in front
of me.

*(**ANYA** enters and a single spotlight follows
her while she moves to stand next to **WES**.
ANYA and **WES** are both illuminated by their
own spotlight throughout the following.)*

ANYA. It is very very black; one, two, three, four broken
street light; so only little light here tonight. I cannot
think of anything but the words. Just them over and

over. I think maybe if I go to Tottenham Court Road, maybe then. Wes will shout I know but he doesn't feel the strong feeling she gives me; like my heart will explode. I am walking fast but, and I cannot say why but sometime, you know there is the feeling, when you know someone is there. I don't think it is the footsteps I hear first, I don't think it is that. Not then anyway. But I turn around to see because I feel something, and there he is.

WES. First night I saw her in the club there was something in the way she moved. Each movement fluid but certain. Yeah she was fit, really fit, course I saw that straight off, but it wasn't just that. Even then, there was something, though I didn't know anythin' about her. It was practically pitch black that night so I only caught a glimpse as she turned her head to look at me, right at me, suddenly, like she sensed me watching. Felt my eyes on her even before it happened. There she's done it again, turned her head glancin' back, catchin' me out again; catchin' me glancin', no, not glancin', gazin'. All these months together and I know everything about her, every single bit of her. I don't need no glance back to know it's her. I raise my hand, give her a little wave, shout for her to wait for me.

ANYA. He shakes his hand at me, shouts at me. I cannot see his face but the hand he shakes, it is a black hand. His hand looks angry I think. He is not far now and so I speed up. But when I try to move faster he follows and moves with me. I do not have to turn this time to know. I can feel the, the, what do you say? The (*Thinks a moment.*) The scared. I can feel it in my stomach; it starts small and then grows and grows when I start to hear him behind me. I can hear his shoes now; they hit the ground harder and harder the faster I try to move, I think he is running but I do not dare turn to look.

WES. A weird thing happens then. She moves away from me. I don't really know why. I go after her and have to move quick to keep up.

ANYA. His angry black hand shaking at me. It makes me think of a fist, an angry black fist. Maybe if I had seen his eyes. If he had kind eyes then maybe. But the hood it was hiding his eyes, his face. Mrs Murphy's words are in my head; "these people". From very small I remember my father, my mother saying those words. Aceste personae [these people], they would say over and over, many times when we passed those people in the street back home. Aceste personae [these people], Aceste personae [these people], Aceste personae [these people], and I think of angry black eyes, in an angry black face to go with his angry clenched fist. I look around the street; there is no one else. How can there be no one, this city is full of people? I start to run.

WES. I can hear the blood rushing through my ears. Might have been the whiskey I just downed but I don't think so. This is different, this feeling. I'm moving fast, I know that, but I shouldn't be so out of breathe. I'm fitter than most; a five mile jog round the park, down to the canal, then up to the mosque and back most days. The odd game of five a side in the park if I can round up the lads. OK, so the footie's happenin' less and less now we're all getting' on a bit, in spitting distance of the big 3-0, but this *(***WES*** is breathless. It is clear he is having trouble getting his breath.* **WES** *puts his hand to his chest.)* I try to call out to Anya for her to stop but I ain't got the breath for it.

ANYA. I run as fast as I can but I know there is no use. I can hear his breath every one now. Loud, heavy, quick; like when Wes had wheezing in Christmas time. I feel it, he is right there; if I turn he will be on top of me. Even so I don't stop. A hand on mine, his hand grabbing my arm. Stopping me. I cannot stop the scream that comes but it is quiet, quieter than I mean it to be. I cannot make my body do what I want tonight.

WES. I gently take her arm, laughing through gasping breaths, trying to stop her running.

ANYA. I struggle with him, he pulls off his hood. I stop struggling.

WES. *(Still breathless.)* Her tiny little scream stops my laughter. The fear in it, her struggle against me until my hood is down and her eyes are on mine, stops my laughter.

ANYA. That look; his eyes see inside, see everything. I feel like I am standing on this street corner naked.

WES. She doesn't look away, not even for a moment. I can see her willing me to unsee that flash of something I just caught in her that wasn't meant for my eyes.

(**WES** *really begins to struggle to breathe.*)

ANYA. Wes?

WES. I *(has no breath to say more.)*

ANYA. Come on.

WES. She says. Demonstrating steady even breathes. Tapping out four beats for each one.

ANYA. He stops breathing, just for a moment. Stands looking at me; completely still. Like one of those winding toys you give children.

(*The individual spotlights merge into one shared spotlight which illuminates both* **ANYA** *and* **WES.**)

WES. Slowly I pick up her rhythm and I can catch my breath.

ANYA AND WES. *(Together.)* In; one, two, three four. Out; one, two, three, four.

WES. I am embarrassed but she doesn't seem to be.

ANYA. I am ashamed but he seems hurt.

WES. I drop my gaze, she doesn't. I can feel it on me.

ANYA. I have to look away.

> *(**WES** and **ANYA** are no longer voicing a monologue in the following but are speaking directly to one another.)*

WES. Anya –

ANYA. Wes, I am sorry.

WES. I think of the flash of something I caught.

ANYA. Look, I saw a black man running –

WES. Black?

ANYA. No I mean, I saw a man running to me in the dark and –

WES. You said black.

ANYA. No, I meant a man only, a man, any man running to me in the night. Is it wrong I was the scared? Anyone would be scared, yes?

WES. But black was important.

ANYA. No, a mistake I said only.

WES. Must've been important or you wouldn't have said it.

ANYA. Wes?

WES. How much of it was the black in me that made you run, made you scream, made you terrified?

ANYA. But Wes?

WES. But Anya?

(**WES** *is horrified. He pulls up his hood.* **WES** *and* **ANYA** *watch each other.*)

(*Beat.*)

(*Lights down.*)

Scene Thirteen

*(Lights up. Friday. It is early morning and so **DAWN** is just breaking throughout the scene. **JT** and **CHERISE** are at a sports complex in Hampstead, London. They are doing some training exercises, during their training session. Behind them a set of portable hurdles are set up. **JT** and **CHERISE** do some stretches and lunges for a short period as they speak.)*

CHERISE. Takin' no notice. Still messin' around like I'm one of the boys. State of me, all this make up; I look like / a clown.

JT. /Gorgeous. Never go for me, not in a million years. Not lookin' like that.

CHERISE. Called for me this mornin'. First time he did that, proper gentleman, carried my bag an all.

JT. My hands were sweatin'.

CHERISE. No waitin' at the bus station for him today.

*(To **JT**.)* Ready are ya?

JT. *(To **CHERISE**.)* Course. Gotta be. Today's everything.

Thought she'd laugh when she opened the front door and saw me standin' there. She didn't. She just kinda smiled in a way I hadn't seen before. I meant to do it then but she just looked so *(Does not have the words to describe it adequately.)* You know?

CHERISE. Look at him; in his own world. Concentratin' so hard I don't even register. Standin' up straight, straighter than I ever seen him. Right at the start, on the line, leaning forward slightly as he waits for the one, two, three and he's off; blastin' over them hurdles like he got a devil chasin' him.

JT. A flash of blue.

CHERISE. But I don't mind. What did I expect? It's JT and one thing I know about JT is he's all about the focus up here. (**CHERISE** *touches her head.*)

JT. Corner of my eye and I catch it, her blue top, but only just. Speed I'm takin' these hurdles most of the world's a blur. But I can feel her; she's right along with me, managin' to keep up, though I'm goin' like the wind.

CHERISE. What would he see in me? He's clever –

JT. The heat from her body –

CHERISE. Fit, knows what he wants –

JT. I can't help but be aware of her coz she's matchin' me now, jumpin' with me, hurdle for hurdle.

CHERISE. And then we're fallin'. JT misjudges, brings down the next hurdle and me with him.

JT. I struggle trying to break my fall and catch Cherise all in the same motion.

CHERISE. JT's there to break my fall and I lay in his arms for the briefest moment until he springs from me as if I were radioactive and tries to do the couldn't give a toss brush off.

JT. (*To* **CHERISE.**) Can't all sit around.

CHERISE. (*To* **JT.**) Can we not?

> (**CHERISE** *pulls* **JT** *down to the track beside her and the two laugh as he lands with a bump by her side.*)

JT. (*To* **CHERISE.**) Cherise?

CHERISE. (*To* **JT.**) Yeah?

> (*Beat.*)

JT. Ask her, come on. What's the worst she can say? Ask her, ask her, ask her. *(To* **CHERISE**.*)* Dad's buildin' a trophy cabinet.

Oh nice one, really smooth.

CHERISE. *(To* **JT**.*)* That's, um, well, nice I s'pose.

JT. For me I mean, all the ones in the hall cupboard and –

CHERISE. One from today.

JT. Won't be a trophy, just a medal if –

CHERISE. When. A medal like that, nothin' just about it. Can still put a medal in a trophy cabinet.

JT. Yeah?

CHERISE. Yeah.

JT. Dad's obsessed with it, hammerin' away most nights, surprised no one's complained.

CHERISE. Nan did. Told her to just bang on the wall and you guys'd get the message but she said it ain't lady like. She put a four-page letter about it under your door. Spent ages at the kitchen table writin'. I think your mom's making us some cupcakes as a compromise.

JT. She is?

CHERISE. Yeah, Nan said. How is your mom?

    (Beat.)

JT. Think I can do it today? Get a spot on the team?

CHERISE. Know you can. Anyway I'll be there watchin' to see everyone's faces when you smash it.

JT. You got school.

CHERISE. But –

JT. It's all the way in Surrey; no way you can make it there and back in your dinner hour.

CHERISE. It's one day JT.

JT. You start waggin' again and they're gonna kick you out. You get kicked out of school you ain't doin' your exams. What'd your Nan say then; she'd send you back to your mom for sure.

CHERISE. You sound like Nan you know that?

>   *(Beat.)*

Your dad comin' to watch then?

JT. Wouldn't miss it he says.

CHERISE. Your mom she goin' too?

JT. Why?

CHERISE. Just wondered.

>   *(Beat.)*

You never talk about her.

JT. You don't talk about your mom either. I don't get on you about that.

CHERISE. Mine hasn't been gone for months and months.

JT. She's been away OK, so what? She went on holiday and now she's back.

CHERISE. Holiday?

JT. Yes, holiday.

CHERISE. For nearly nine months?

JT. Eight months OK. Eight months three days.

CHERISE. JT?

>   *(Beat.)*

What Marcus and Darren were on about yesterday –

JT. Those two clowns don't know anythin'.

CHERISE. Neither do I coz you never say.

> (**CHERISE** *shivers slightly.*)

JT. *(Picking up his hooded top.)* Go on put that on before you freeze to death.

> (**CHERISE** *puts* **JT***'s hooded top on.*)

CHERISE. JT?

JT. Yeah?

CHERISE. That holiday, one your mom went on, I'm glad she's back.

> (**JT** *considers confiding in* **CHERISE** *a moment but then thinks better of it. He begins doing sit ups.*)

JT. *(To* **CHERISE***.)* Gotta get this done.

Concentrate.

CHERISE. JT?

> (**JT** *jumps up and begins to shadow box.*)

JT. Concentrate. Just you against the bar, no one else, just yourself to push, to better, to coax, to nudge a little bit further each time. 2 metres 4; that's where I'm aimin'; and I can do it, I know; just give me time and I'm up there, watch.

CHERISE. I'll see you then.

> (**CHERISE** *begins gathering up her things and starts taking off* **JT***'s hooded top.*)

JT. *(Grabs* **CHERISE***'s arm.)* Don't.

> (**CHERISE** *tries to shake* **JT** *off her but he holds on.*)

CHERISE. Loose me.

JT. *(He pulls his hooded top back onto* **CHERISE** *and zips it up.)* Keep it; don't want you to catch cold do I?

CHERISE. Like you said, I got school.

JT. Nah, know what? you're right; what's one day?

CHERISE. Don't want to give them an excuse to kick me out do I?

> *(***CHERISE** *finishes gathering her things and goes to leave.)*

JT. *(Trying to take her bag from her.)* Let me help?

CHERISE. *(Grabbing the bag away from him.)* You're alright.

> *(***CHERISE** *leaves.)*

JT. *(Calling after her.)* Cherise?

> *(Lights down, as* JT *hurriedly gathers up the portable hurdles and the rest of his stuff to go after* **CHERISE.***)*

Scene Fourteen

(Lights up. Friday morning. It is still very early; the sun has only just come up. **WES** *and* **ANYA**'s *flat. They have been fighting all night.* **WES** *paces as* **ANYA** *sits in a chair and cannot look him in the eye.)*

ANYA. I can't keep say it.

WES. So don't.

ANYA. Then what?

WES. I don't know.

*(***ANYA*** gets up and puts her arms around* **WES**'s *neck. This stills his pacing and* **ANYA** *meets his eyes for the first time.)*

ANYA. Wes –

WES. *(Taking her arms from around his neck and moving away from* **ANYA.** *He is very distressed.)* Don't OK? Please.

(Beat.)

You tell me, if you had turned around –

ANYA. It nothing to do with that, you –

WES. It was you, you said it. If you'd turned around and I hadn't been black, would you have run?

ANYA. Wes, you know me.

WES. Do I?

ANYA. You know.

WES. Thought I did.

ANYA. I keep say if I know it is you I would not run but the hood –

WES. That doesn't make it better.

ANYA. You are not fair. Anyone in the street in the night they see a black man run to them, his hood up and they feel the scared.

WES. See there it is again. Not a man, any man but a black man. You're not like that. Not the you who I've known all this time. Months and weeks and days of knowing you and I never saw that in you, not once.

ANYA. I am tired Wes, all night we go round and round; the sun it is up and I don't know what I say I am so tired. I say black but I don't mean it.

WES. What do you mean?

>	*(Beat.)*

If that's really what you think why are you with me?

>	*(The sound of a hairdryer takes us from* **WES** *and* **ANYA***'s flat to* **MISS B***'s living room.* **CHERISE** *is finishing drying her hair.)*

MISS B. *(Unplugging the hair dryer at the wall.)* How much time mi fi tell yuh seh nuh duh dis inna di living room.

CHERISE. I was bein' careful. Put a towel down and everything. *(Begrudgingly clearing up her hair things.)* Thanks Nan, gonna be late now.

MISS B. Ah who fault dat? Yuh an dat bwoy runnin roun, only God knows where all mawnin, an now ah mi ago mek yuh late?

CHERISE. It's just a bit of hair Nan. Look I'll get a brush, sweep up the bits that dropped. Just a few strands.

MISS B. Few? ...luk pon di ole heap ah hair pon di carpet! ... Weh yuh seh yuh sweep up? Weh dem deh?

CHERISE. Gotta leave in ten minutes or I would, but when I get back from school you see if I don't.

MISS B. Ah suppose yuh feel yuh maid wi duh it fi yuh in di mean time!

> (**MISS B** *makes a big show of getting down on her hands and knees and starting to pick up bits of* **CHERISE**'s *hair off the floor.*)

Like shi duh everything else fi yuh?

CHERISE. Alright, Alright, I hear you. Get up Nanny; I'll get the brush; I'll do it now.

> (**MISS B** *has exaggerated somewhat about the amount of hair and after the first few moments she has to really hunt for strands of hair to pick up.*)

MISS B. *(Calling after* **CHERISE** *as she gets the brush from out on the balcony.)* Yeah, yuh hear mi Cherise... Yuh always hear mi, but yuh eva listen?

> (*The sound of a busy London street during the rush hour; traffic, people calling out to one another etc.*)

CHERISE. And I'm on the balcony and there he is down below, like somehow he knew I would be. I watch him a moment struggling with all them hurdles and his ridiculous bag that's always just a little bit too full. He calls up to me from the street but I'm still seethin'.

JT. This one's on the ignore him 'til he gets the message I reckon. The silent treatment 'til I see the error of my ways. But she ain't gonna phase me; I ain't in the mood for the dance she's proposin', not with the trials later and the load I got on my back and all the crazy I gotta deal with back home.

> *(Calling up to* **CHERISE**.*)* You wanna go out or what?

CHERISE. And just like that, he's got my attention.

JT. You and me after. Today six o'clock, Nando's on the high street?

CHERISE. Six months and nothin', then boom, he's right there in the middle of the street not carin' who's watchin'. Couldn't help it; I was tryin' to play it cool but I was grinnin' like an idiot.

And I'm turnin' to him, shoutin' back "what d'ya say?" like I ain't heard just so I can hear him ask me again; so everyone in the flats can hear him. I'm raisin' my hand to wave but then it's down again and I'm shoutin' for JT to watch out with all that I've got. I can see them comin' up behind him but he's got his eyes on me and he ain't clocked the threat.

>*(The sound of* **WES** *playing a song in the style of Miles Davis'* [**"SANCTUARY"**]* *perfectly.)*

ANYA. Talk to me.

>*(**WES** ignores her and continues playing.)*

Wes?

>*(**WES** continues playing until **ANYA** grabs his sheet music and he stops abruptly.)*

WES. What you doin'?

ANYA. What you thinking?

WES. You don't wanna know trust me.

---

* A licence to produce CITY MELODIES does not include a performance licence for "SANCTUARY". The publisher and author suggest that the licensee contact PRS to ascertain the music publisher and contact such music publisher to license or acquire permission for performance of the song. If a licence or permission is unattainable for "SANCTUARY", the licensee may not use the song in CITY MELODIES but should create an original composition in a similar style or use a similar song in the public domain. For further information, please see Music Use Note on page iii.

(Beat.)

And I dart at her, tryin' to get my sheets but she's runnin'. Quick she is, too fast for me.

ANYA. I run for it. Balcony the only place I can go but he's comin' fast and I promise, it wasn't deliberate, but I slip, have to grip the railing to keep from go over side. Papers drop.

WES. Sheet music's tumblin' down into the street and the look she's givin' me.

ANYA. The way he stares.

WES. She's scared. Of me. That rocks me, to the core of me.

(To **ANYA**.*)* You wanna know what I'm thinkin' now? What are you scared of? Don't you know me?

(Beat.)

See last night when you left that message, about that Murphy woman, I thought you'd be home. Like we said, you know, no more goin' to that place but comin' home instead and we'd sort it together. Was gonna head home after the knock back on the audition when Maria called, said she'd been tryin' all day but couldn't get through to your phone. Gave me a message for you. "Your letters from home are pilin' up", she said. "You need to come and get them as soon as". After that Maria and I had a little chat about –

ANYA. What she tell you?

WES. All your letters came here I thought. Why's your family still sendin' your letters to Maria's?

ANYA. Wes you don't understand.

WES. See then I didn't think too much about it. But now I am, now I can't get the why of it off my mind.

ANYA. Wes, does that matter? It's nothing.

WES. Is that why you didn't want your family to visit?

ANYA. Wes don't.

WES. Do they even know about me?

ANYA. Yes, I tell them, it's just *(She cannot say.)*

WES. Well that's funny, coz according to Maria they think you two still share a place.

ANYA. Wes it's not easy for me. They only know how things are in Romania; they don't know how it is in London.

WES. Am I the reason they can't visit?

ANYA. They don't know people like you.

WES. What's so different about me?

ANYA. Wes?

WES. Go on tell me, what is it?

ANYA. You know what is this. I know what is this.

WES. Say it!

ANYA. Why? Does it matter what they would think? Is more important what I think.

WES. It matters you didn't tell me, wouldn't have if Maria hadn't phoned.

ANYA. Wes some people –

WES. Your people.

ANYA. Don't be like that.

WES. Can you hear that?

(Sound of a phone ringing.)

DAWN. *(Answering the phone.)* Yes?

CHERISE. Mom?

DAWN. Cherise?

CHERISE. They've knocked him down Mom, Nan won't let me out.

DAWN. What is it love?

CHERISE. Right there, outside your window, you can get to him, help him.

DAWN. But baby I *(Cannot continue.)*

CHERISE. Can't you hear it Mom? Do somethin' Mom.

DAWN. Alright baby, alright.

MISS B. Dawn, yuh nuh get yuhself mix up inna nutten, yuh hear mi?

CHERISE. But Nanny?

MISS B. Cherise mi love, wat yuh really kno bout dat bwoy? ... Listen tuh weh him ah seh... dat soun like anything gud tuh yuh? Nuh only gun man chat suh.

CHERISE. Nanny, can't you hear that?

MISS B. Call di police pickney, yuh naaa set foot outta mi sight.

> *(The line goes dead. Throughout the following the dialling of 999 can be heard and then the number ringing.)*

DAWN. I meant to I really did. To go out there; tell them off, tell them I knew their mothers, anything to stop the sound of fist connecting with bone, the thump of shoes stomping on flesh and tissue and organs and ribs and neck bones and skull.

CHERISE. *(Into the phone as soon as it is answered,)* Hello police, you gotta hurry.

DAWN. But God forgive me, I draw my curtains, cover my ears and wait for the wail of sirens to relieve me from having to be the one.

ANYA. *(Looking over the balcony to the street below.)* What are they doing?

WES. *(Also looking down to the three boys in the street below.)* You already know don't you? Black boy like that with his two hoodie wearin' mates; must be up to no good.

ANYA. That not fair.

WES. Never mind that's the kid who borrowed my limited edition *Bitches Brew* LP and brought it back in pristine condition.

ANYA. Stop it.

WES. Never mind that's the kid from upstairs that's always down the gym or off playin' some sport or other somewhere with all that equipment he's always carryin'. All that you can see is how terrifying he is right? How his blackness makes him scarey?

> (**WES** *realises there is something wrong with what he is witnessing below.*)

(Shouting down to the boys.) Oi you, leave him alone!

ANYA. *(To* **WES.***)* You think I am scared of him? Does this look like I am scared to you?

WES. *(To* **ANYA.***)* Anya stop, what are you doing? *(Shouting to the boys.)* Alright lads, that's enough!

ANYA. And then I'm running, not really thinking, just want to prove to him.

WES. And she's out of the flat and flying down the stairs.

ANYA. He's telling me to stop. Doesn't think I will.

WES. Problem is I know she won't back down now; she thinks she's got something to prove.

CHERISE. I can hear the sirens. Not close enough.

MISS B. Mi lock har up inna di house, but mi di affi look outside, fi jus si what ah gwaan... Mi jus si dem back part like, two ah dem... dem neva big.

DAWN. I hear running feet in the corridor right outside my door. I realise my whole body's shaking.

WES. She bursts out the front door just ahead of me.

MISS B. Jus two bwoy... two white bwoy weh mi si already... Two bwoy weh stan up against ah wall an laf afta ah ole Jamaican cook, becausa how shi talk... an nuhbody neva seh nutten.

ANYA. But I am scared now. Very scared. He is not moving, this boy. This little black boy who one time, he ask me about Miles, which one I rated most. He hear me playing him in the lift, headphones are too loud. We both agree *Bitches Brew* best one. Nothing else touch that one. Now all I can do is hold him and wait. I hear like an ambulance is coming and pray it come soon.

WES. I get there too late and can only hold her as she rocks him.

DAWN. A wailing starts up; a woman in the street outside my window. I cannot bear the sound, it gives me goose bumps and I run to the bathroom to be sick.

CHERISE. *(Shouting down from her balcony to* **JT** *in the street.)* Yes JT! 'Course I will! You and me, today 6 o'clock, Nando's on the high street! And I wanna see your medal yeah!

> *(Lights down as the sound of police cars and an ambulance approaching can be heard.)*

Scene Fifteen

(Friday, late afternoon. **MISS B** *has baked two fruit cakes. They are on the table in front of her, one is iced and she has a bowl with a tiny bit of icing sugar in it beside her.)*

MISS B. *(Sizing up the amount of icing left in the bowl.)* No sah, dis nuh look enough, weh yuh think Cherry?

CHERISE. –

MISS B. First mi di ah think she fi jus bake one big one... di biggest mi Eva duh. Cause yuh kno how him like cake... den mi seh ah betta mi jus duh two, cause den can cut up an share.

CHERISE. –

MISS B. Everybody like ah nice piece ah fruit cake.

*(***CHERISE*** watches* **MISS B** *for a moment.)*

CHERISE. You been next door yet? Coz I have and *(***CHERISE*** stops herself.)* Nevermind.

MISS B. Jus mek mi smooth dis out, it nuh straight. *(***MISS B*** starts meticulously smoothing out the icing on the first cake so it is exactly even and level.)*

CHERISE. I'm gonna miss the noise; all that bangin'. Got used to it after a while. JT's dad ain't got no trophy cabinet to be buildin' now does he?

MISS B. Pass mi di knife deh.

CHERISE. *(Hands* **MISS B** *a palette knife that is near her.)* Nan, how can you just *(***CHERISE*** stops herself again.)* I ain't seen you go next door?

MISS B. Dat ah fi mi business.

(Beat.)

Mi wi dweet.

CHERISE. When?

MISS B. Wen mi ready.

CHERISE. You scared?

(Beat.)

I was. Terrified they'd ask me; want to know, 'why didn't you do something, anything', just –

MISS B. Mi wi si dem ah di set-up tonight.

CHERISE. Told them I tried but –

MISS B. Mi ah mek dem yah fi di set-up... him always use tuh tek piece carry ome wen him come ere. Guh dung ah di shop fi mi, an get some icing sugar.

CHERISE. Oh so you got too much cookin' to do, that it? Or you just hidin' in here?

MISS B. Mine how yuh talk tuh mi.

CHERISE. Or what?

(Beat.)

*(***CHERISE*** grabs the cake that* **MISS B** *has just finished icing so it looks perfect and slowly pulls it to bits as she speaks.)*

Or you'll send me back to live with Mom? I could care less now; she's not the only one with an act from what I can see. Or what? You'll make me stay in the flat and listen to my best friend kicked to death outside with no one to help him? Just coz he don't speak English like you think he should? Just coz in your twisted mind you're judgin' him, thinkin' how he speaks tells you he must be some kind of gangster to be scared of? But really you don't even know a thing about him?

MISS B. Pickney, yuh ah guh get di icing ah di shop ar not?

CHERISE. I've been round there you know. His parents.

His mom doesn't look like cake will do it for her, his dad neither.

MISS B. Is all mi hav tuh give.

CHERISE. JT's mom's goin' back on holiday after the vigil she said.

MISS B. Might be fi di best... guh bout har business likkle.

CHERISE. So you don't have to see her? Tell her what you heard? What you did?

>   *(Beat.)*

MISS B. Ah mi did wrong. Yuh think seh mi nuh kno dat?

CHERISE. Did you know I'm on for an A maybe even an A* in my English now? All 'coz of JT helpin' me, 'coz he didn't want anyone callin' me dickhead? 'Coz he wanted me lookin' up for once? That's how gangster he was Nan.

MISS B. Cherise, dat language, yuh use tu yuh grandmother... mi/

CHERISE. What?

MISS B. *(Thinks better of it.)* Nutten dear, nuh worry.

>   *(**MISS B** is unsure if she will let her but
>   she takes one of **CHERISE**'s hands in hers.
>   **CHERISE** lets her.)*

Guh get di icing fi mi nuh man?

>   *(**MISS B** takes a £20 note from her purse and
>   holds it out to **CHERISE**.)*

Di vanilla one, wid di butta cream. An get ah likkle something fi yuhslf tuh darling...whateva yuh want... yuh nuh affi carry back nuh change.

(After a brief hesitation **CHERISE** *takes the money.)*

(Lights down.)

Scene Sixteen

(Lights up. Friday evening, about eight o'clock. A single spotlight picks out **ANYA** *only.)*

ANYA. Wes not understand; he can't. How he understand? His English very good so he don't know this.

Almost a year I am here now and still days and days if I not need things, no work, I stay inside. Easier I think. But today I am in the small shop again across from my building; near to the lights and next to the place for jobs. Just to buy for supper. Cheese, onions and two *(Thinks for a moment.)* you know? *(Thinks again but just cannot get the word.)* Always this one I don't remember. Um, what can I say? Yellow, like the oranges but the sour one. *(Closes her eyes a moment to try to find the word.)* two, two, ah, I don't remember.

Man in shop he say something, I am at the till and he smile and then say something. But I don't know what is this he say so I look at him, I ask him; "repeat please?" Then he get that look he always have with me, slight smiling mouth, but not happy smiling, smiling in a different way, a way I know by now, a way I have seen many times in London. I hate that look.

Then the man like always he talk loud to me and slow like I am child. He come in my face, close; I can smell his breath, it smell of mint and cigarettes and garlic and onions. He speaks more and more loud when I can't understand.

I get embarrass now so I leave my things, just on the counter and I walk away. Cheese, onions and two yellow things like orange but sour. I just leave them there. This man, the one who always gives me that slight smiling look that makes me want to stay quiet, he shout after me. The words he shouts; those I know, those I have hear many times. *(Shouting.)* "Why don't you people learn bloody English?"

"You people" and I think of aceste personae [these people], and of running from Wes because of what I have in my head about aceste personae [these people] from way back. Aceste personae [these people] is in all of us I am thinking, not Mrs Murphy only. When she say it to me, I worry, I angry very very much, I think she unfair; like she open a box and put all things in it from things she hear, things she think, things people tell her about people like me. So when she meet a Romanian she just open her box and put me in thinking she know all about aceste personae [these people]. But she know nothing not really, she don't ask me only tell me this is you, I know you from this box I have so I don't have to ask you nothing. I think maybe Wes feel this when I run.

I look at the shop man and think how I never want to be like him. I know my face is coming red and so I put my head down and start to walk out.

But then this girl she –

(Another spotlight now picks out **CHERISE**.*)*

CHERISE. Oi, who you callin' you people? *(To* **ANYA**.*)* You really gonna just leave your stuff?

ANYA. She speak up for me. *(To* **CHERISE**.*)* Why?

CHERISE. Just.

    (Beat.)

Saw you this mornin'.

ANYA. The boy? I try but –

CHERISE. JT, that's his name.

ANYA. Well thank you for –

CHERISE. You goin' to the vigil tonight?

ANYA. My boyfriend he wants to.

CHERISE. You don't?

ANYA. I don't know.

CHERISE. See, I don't think JT'd want it. I mean I think he would in a way, people thinkin' of him, somewhere for his parents to go and that but doesn't feel exactly right for him, you know? JT had belief, he was gonna do somethin' big, I knew it, he knew it. This vigil thing seems so ordinary, so quiet, respectful.

ANYA. You do not want to be respectful?

CHERISE. No, yes, I don't know. JT, he doesn't like being put in a box; doin' a thing just coz people expect that from you, you know?

ANYA. I talk to JT one time only; we argued about music.

CHERISE. Miles Davis?

ANYA. *(Surprised.)* Yes.

CHERISE. Drove me mad with it.

> *(The sound of* **WES** *playing a song in the style of Miles Davis'* **["SANCTUARY"]** *on his trumpet is heard from nearby and continues until the end of the scene.)*

ANYA. My boyfriend drives me crazy with him too.

---

* A licence to produce CITY MELODIES does not include a performance licence for "SANCTUARY". The publisher and author suggest that the licensee contact PRS to ascertain the music publisher and contact such music publisher to license or acquire permission for performance of the song. If a licence or permission is unattainable for "SANCTUARY", the licensee may not use the song in CITY MELODIES but should create an original composition in a similar style or use a similar song in the public domain. For further information, please see Music Use Note on page iii.

CHERISE. Oh no, JT wasn't my boyfrie— (**CHERISE** *does not finish the thought.*)

ANYA. What?

CHERISE. Nothing. Nevermind. Sometimes crazy is good though. Sometimes a little bit of crazy is the most conducive thing, you know, to keeping you sane.

ANYA. Cond, conduc; I do not know this word.

CHERISE. Sorry. Conducive: making a certain situation or outcome likely or possible. On for an A in English me.

ANYA. Ah this is good.

CHERISE. 'Spose. Seen you around the flats. Could help you with your English. I mean, if you want.

ANYA. Why?

CHERISE. What?

ANYA. Why offer this?

CHERISE. Coz.

ANYA. This is not good reason I think, and I am stranger to you.

CHERISE. So?

ANYA. But I must pay you some money for this, yes?

CHERISE. Don't want no money from ya.

(*Beat.*)

Hate guys like him, that's all. JT was right; always used to say, "don't let people call you a dick head, or put you in a box". (*Thinks for a brief moment.*) I'm gonna be a teacher, wanna be anyway. No not wanna be, I'm gonna be. Teach English and that. So really you'd be like practise for me.

ANYA. So I am guinea pig?

CHERISE. If you like.

ANYA. Let me give you something then? Please?

CHERISE. And she did. Got me a rocket from the little shop; asked her for the biggest one she could get. Must have been more than the change I had after Nan's icing, but she never said.

ANYA. I stood with the girl in front of our building, the firework went up but I think maybe it is faulty.

CHERISE. Could see her face, all compassion and wonderin' how I was gonna react to the dud.

ANYA. But then –

CHERISE. Then –

ANYA. Boom!

CHERISE. It exploded, lit up the night so many different colours. Woke people up.

DAWN. The noise of it.

CHERISE. Twitching net curtain from mom's front room.

MISS B. As soon as mi hear di noise mi run come.

WES. Peek over the balcony just in time to hear it, see the last of the glow. Anya setting off fireworks in the courtyard with some girl.

ANYA. Wes's hanging over the balcony playing his heart out.

CHERISE. Tune. Yeah this is right. Really right. JT never looked down, not a day in his life. He only ever looked up and saw where he was going.

ANYA. A dreamer?

CHERISE. Not just a dreamer, he had plans.

ANYA. Someone tell me one time that you have to have dreams.

CHERISE. He was supposed to be jumpin'.

(The sound of banging coming from the flats begins; as **JT**'s *dad continues building the trophy cabinet.)*

ANYA. Sometime it hard, very hard to keep looking up but you must. (**ANYA** *squeezes* **CHERISE**'s *hand.*) I am music teacher and even when the notes are not sound right and the melody sound like many elephants I keep on playing, again and again until the music sound better and after time it sound like I dream it would.

CHERISE. Yeah?

ANYA. Yes.

*(***DAWN*** comes in behind ***ANYA*** and ***CHERISE***. She is holding ***JT***'s cap.)*

CHERISE. It's just so weird; JT not, not *(Cannot say it.)*

DAWN. I know baby.

*(***CHERISE*** looks up at ***DAWN*** in surprise.)*

CHERISE. There was no make-up maskin' it, no clone in a business suit, no not a strand out of place hairdo between me and her. First time in two years I'd seen her drop the act. Don't think I'd seen her in tracksuit bottoms in my life.

Mom?

DAWN. *(To* **CHERISE**.) Baby?

(Beat.)

Sorry.

CHERISE. Y'alright mom?

DAWN. I should be asking you that.

(DAWN tentatively gives CHERISE her cap back.)

Kept it then?

CHERISE. For a bit. Gave it away in the end. Looked better on JT.

(CHERISE places JT's cap on top of the few bouquets that have been placed at the front of the building.)

In the end I gave it to him. Coz he liked it and I liked that I had somethin' I could give him.

(CHERISE puts the hood up on the hooded sweatshirt that JT gave her and smooths down the front of it.)

Gave me this. I was freezin'. Tried to look after me a bit.

DAWN. I like it.

CHERISE. Yeah?

DAWN. Yeah.

(Lights down completely on DAWN and CHERISE. Lights up on ANYA and MISS B.)

ANYA. *(ANYA stares at MISS B but is a little unsure.)* I know you I think?

MISS B. *(To ANYA.)* Yuh kno, wen mi si yuh dis mawnin mi did kno seh mi kno yuh from sumweh... Ah jus now it come tuh mi... Yuh get yuh telephone vice yet?

ANYA. I still working on that.

(MISS B hugs ANYA tight.)

MISS B. Yuh know weh mi fine out, mi darlin... Telephone vice ah nuh everything. As long as yuh can talk

Henglish gud, suh dat people can understan wat yuh seh... Afta telephone vice nuh real.

ANYA. Acting?

MISS B. Yeah, fi fool people, mek dem think dem kno yuh, wen dem nuh kno yuh at all. Wat ah ting, how people, who fi kno betta, have seen ah likkle life, can tink seh dem kno smady, jus from how dem talk Henglish... God help mi, it took ah hard lesson fi mi fi learn dat.

*(Lights down as **WES** plays a song in the style of Miles Davis' [**"SANCTUARY"**]* and **JT***'s dad hammers away at the trophy cabinet he is making.)*

The End

---

* A licence to produce CITY MELODIES does not include a performance licence for "SANCTUARY". The publisher and author suggest that the licensee contact PRS to ascertain the music publisher and contact such music publisher to license or acquire permission for performance of the song. If a licence or permission is unattainable for "SANCTUARY", the licensee may not use the song in CITY MELODIES but should create an original composition in a similar style or use a similar song in the public domain. For further information, please see Music Use Note on page iii.

ABOUT THE AUTHOR

Lorna French is a playwright, writing workshop leader and dramaturg. Lorna has most recently presented a reading of *Esther* at Jermyn Street Theatre in March 2022. *Jacaranda* was produced by Pentabus Theatre and Theatre by the Lake for a tour of rural venues in 2021. She also wrote for Limbik Theatre and the HearMe Now monologue series (via Titilola Dawudu and Tamasha Theatre Company) in 2021. She wrote the short play *I See You Now*, produced as part of the 15 Heroines plays at Jermyn Street Theatre in November 2020. Also the short radio drama *NFA* for Menagerie Theatre Company and the University of Cambridge in October 2020. *Esther*, a play about Black African Caribbean women of Birmingham and the West Midlands, was inspired by oral history interviews with several local women. It was shortlisted for the Theatre Uncut Political Playwriting Award 2020 and longlisted for the Women's Prize for Playwriting 2020. Esther received a staged reading at Midlands Arts Centre (MAC) in 2019 made possible by a Developing Your Creative Practice award from Arts Council England.

Other past work includes *The Last Flag*, a co-written Afternoon Drama for BBC Radio 4 and Eclipse Theatre Company in 2018 and a co-written adaptation of *Jane Eyre* for Bolton Octagon, also in 2018. In 2017, Lorna wrote a one-act play called *Transitions* for Birmingham Rep Education Department and RSA Academy. In 2016, she wrote an audio drama called *You Say* for the White Open Spaces monologues co-commissioned by Eclipse and Pentabus Theatre. Lorna is a two-time winner of the Alfred Fagon Award (in 2006 and 2016) and has presented work at, or written work for, Birmingham Rep, Oval House, MAC, Young Vic and New Wolsey Theatre.

Lorna is currently mentoring a writer for Red Talent Management and also working with the National Theatre's Education Department on New Views. This involves working with young people writing plays in secondary schools in the Midlands and London. She is also working as a Lead Writer for Writing West Midlands running monthly Sparks writing workshops with young people. She has previously worked as an Associate Lecturer on the Writing for Performance MA and other BA Performing Arts Undergraduate programmes at the University of Derby. She has also worked as a dramaturg on *Close to the Edge* by Viv Manjaro (Planet Arts and Red Earth Collective) and on *Revealed* by Daniel Anderson (Rites of Passage Productions).

Lightning Source UK Ltd.
Milton Keynes UK
UKHW021814140722
405868UK00010B/965

9 780573 133558